re:generation Europe

Floris de Witte

re:generation Europe

Ten Proposals for Another Europe

Floris de Witte
Department of Law
London School of Economics and Political Science
London, UK

ISBN 978-3-030-19787-2   ISBN 978-3-030-19788-9   (eBook)
https://doi.org/10.1007/978-3-030-19788-9

This Palgrave Macmillan imprint is published by the registered company Springer Nature
Switzerland AG
The registered company address is: Gewerbestrasse 11, 6330 Cham, Switzerland

To Oskar and his friends

ACKNOWLEDGEMENTS

I owe a great debt to my friend Moritz Hartmann. It was in November 2011, in the early morning in a Berlin bar called *Zu Dir oder Zu Mir?*, that we realized that we shared a similar view on the EU's future. That view was one based on incredulity: that the continent that we both love is run as if it were a technocratic, austerity-driven monolith. Moritz suggested we write down our ideas and publish them somewhere. I think there might even be a coaster or napkin with some ideas sketched out. Needless to say, I had forgotten most of this when I woke up the next day. As I passed by Moritz' place the day after, however, he sat me down on the kitchen table and told me how we would transform our ideas into something else. And thus *re:generation Europe* was born. In its first years, the project changed shape: it was a manifesto, it was a public project, it was a research network. And then our lives took over, and the project (if not the ideas) fizzled out.

Years later, as I sat down to write this short book, I realized that our ideas were still compelling to me: they resisted the changing times and offered a powerful way to understand the present and future of the integration project. Moritz kindly accepted me stealing many of our joint ideas for this book. If this book is in your hands, it is largely thanks to Moritz' ideas, generosity, and friendship.

I would also like to thank Ambra Finotello, at Palgrave Macmillan. She saw the potential in this project from the start and has encouraged me throughout. Many thanks as well to the Dr. A.H. Heineken Foundation for History for kindly allowing me to republish the *Eurotopia* map.

A final thanks to Pauline and Oskar. Nothing has motivated me more in working on this project than our future together.

CONTENTS

CHAPTER 1

Introduction

Like many stories about the future of European integration, this one starts in Berlin. On 9 November 2011, to be precise, when I sat in the audience at the *Haus der Berliner Festspiele* while José Manuel Barroso, then president of the European Commission, gave the *State of Europe* speech. This speech was the apotheosis of a large two-day conference, at which academics, politicians, and public figures of all sorts discussed the future of Europe. Sitting in the audience I felt a sort of rising frustration that I hadn't felt since my teenage years—a mix of powerlessness and embarrassment that parents tend to provoke in their 15-year old sons and daughters. I was angry at what these people where doing to Europe, at how they thought about her future, and how helpless I was in stopping any of it from happening. More precisely, I was frustrated with the way they treated my generation—as one which will have to deal with the consequences of austerity, welfare rollback, and a deranged climate—and with their collective inability to imagine something more ambitious, more progressive, or simply *better* for Europe's future.

Years later, in the week immediately following the Brexit vote, I found myself in Berlin once again, this time for a conference on the management of the Euro-zone. The weekend prior to the conference was filled with catching up with friends—and talking about Brexit and the future of Europe. Most of my friends are not particularly politically active. In decades of friendship, we barely ever talked about the EU or Europe. Yet,

© The Author(s) 2020
F. de Witte, *re:generation Europe*,
https://doi.org/10.1007/978-3-030-19788-9_1

on that weekend, many Europeans—including my contemporaries, colleagues, and friends—realised two things.

The first was that the story of European integration *can* end. This might sound a bit daft, but for me and many of my contemporaries, the EU has simply always been part of our lives. Imagining a life without the EU is like imagining a future where there is no internet. The stories of our parents—of carrying different wallets with different currencies for a car trip from Belgium to Italy, of their amazement at the discovery of pizza, or of queuing for hours on the border between Spain and France—are, literally, unimaginable to us. But Brexit brought the contingency of the European project back into full view. The EU is *not* like the internet. It is not something that will always be at our disposal, which will increase in density and allow people to come together. It is something that can *end* if we do not care about it. And even caring about Europe is not enough. We must also *take care* of Europe. Brexit, then, brought a change in mood, in particular with the younger generations. I can see it in my students, my apolitical friends, and the explosion of young activists that are engaging with the future of the EU. If we keep passively consuming the EU, it will not survive another 60 years. The only way to protect the integration project is to actively engage with it.

The second feeling that many contemporaries and friends shared after the Brexit referendum was not unlike the teenage frustration that I had felt years before in the *Haus der Berliner Festspiele*. It was anger at what the EU had become, or, to be more precise, at the way in which it had decided to portray Europe. For our generation, Europe is everywhere: in our classmates, our teammates in the local sports team, in the tourist that asks us for directions, in the food we eat, the football stars we revere, the first holidays with friends, and in the future career, spouse, or life we dream about. Yet, the European Union, which portrays itself as a sort of institutional echo of Europe, is none of this. It does not feel natural but artificial. It does not feel local, and all around us; instead it feels distant and unreachable. And, perhaps most importantly, it does not feel urgent and fresh. It doesn't exude the playfulness, extravagance, and excitement that Europe does. Instead it feels aged, tired, and guarded—anxiously looking over its shoulder to see if anyone is trying to capture it, suspiciously eyeing everyone who comes close.

The EU certainly was a progressive and ambitious project in 1957. But now, over 60 years later, its institutions, processes, and policies are still largely the same, even though the challenges that it faces, the complexity of the world in which it operates, and its salience are larger than ever before. Let's put it this way: if European states had decided in favour of an ambitious institutional structure for cooperation today, they would not have devised the EU as it currently is.

The premise of this book is simple. Like many of my contemporaries, I believe in cooperation. I love Europe, in its glorious diversity, with all its dysfunctional quirks and its surprises. But like many of my contemporaries, I am increasingly dissatisfied with the EU, that is, with *this particular* institutional echo of Europe. Europe is, to put it simply, so much more than the EU is. This book offers a narrative towards *another* Europe. It seeks to argue that the two positions that are currently most popular (from the 'protect the EU against the populists' to 'down with the EU') have both got it wrong. We cannot continue to support the EU as it currently is and blindly expect that it will survive the challenges of the next five decades. If the future of the EU is one in which it tries to defend itself against changes, it will be one full of suspicion and anxiety: it will be one where the EU finally implodes due to inertia and general apathy.

We cannot go the other extreme, either. A future based around nation states 'taking back control' is one big illusion: it is much like David Copperfield 'walking' through the Chinese Wall. With all the good will in the world, there is one big Chinese wall standing in the way of nation state taking back control. The interdependence between the different parts of Europe—in trade, in monetary affairs, in culture, in mobility, in capital movement, outlook of life, and in their place in global affairs—means that any decision in which state A 'takes back control' inevitably leads to state B losing the power to do the same.

We have had a taste of what a Europe run by the national capitals looks like, and it is neither pretty nor sustainable: it is one where walls protect borders, where open antagonism between locals and migrants is the norm, reciprocal recriminations about 'lazy Greeks' and 'Nazi Germans' escalate, and every decision in state A is immediately condemned by its neighbours. If the future of Europe is one where the nation states are in charge, the EU will not implode over the years due to inertia and apathy. But chances are that it will explode.

So what can people like me do? How can we articulate a third narrative, beyond these two lazy alternatives, a vision for *another* Europe: one that celebrates the diversity of Europe, that is forward-looking, and that encourages its citizens to engage with it?

This book tries to build up a new narrative in both a theoretical and a practical way. The first half of the book deals with the theory. It looks at three ideas, and at how they have the potential to transform the EU into something that is more *European*—that is, more sensitive to what it is like to *be* a European today and tomorrow.

The first idea that is discussed is trust. If anything typifies the EU of today, it is the complete distrust between actors. In almost every Member State, political parties from the fringes—both the left and the right—are making electoral gains by articulating distrust. This distrust is spread around quite widely: directed towards the national political elite, the media, the European Union, technocrats, but also towards foreigners—be it in the form of refugees, migrant workers, or governments of other Member States. In recent years, Member States have done things on the basis of this distrust that for decades were unimaginable: the suspension of Greek democracy in the name of austerity was justified because the creditors did not trust the Greek state. The building of border fences in Hungary was justified with reference to the distrust of refugees as well as of the neighbouring states. The decision of an Irish tribunal not to extradite Polish criminals was based on a distrust of the independence of the Polish judiciary. Italy's refusal to allow boats with hundreds of refugees and migrants—barely saved from a death at sea—to dock in its ports was based on a distrust of both the individuals on the boats, but also a distrust of the willingness of the other Member States to help shoulder the burden that the refugee crisis has put on Italy. Brexit, perhaps, was the most explicit articulation of this: the Leave campaign was almost exclusively run on the sentiment of distrust of EU migrants, experts, political elites, and globalisation.

Any regeneration or reimagination of Europe has to start, therefore, by thinking about trust. Trust, as we will see, has an almost magical property: it allows people to cooperate, even though they don't know each other. Distrust does the exact opposite: it inhibits cooperation between strangers. The very first step towards another kind of Europe, therefore, must be to think about how we can improve the trust between Europeans. As we will see in Chap. 3, there is reason for optimism: trust in Europe is in plentiful supply. Trust is generated in a number of ways. Chief among them are cooperating with each other, being exposed to differences, and learning more about each other. Each of these reduces the distrust between citizens because it allows us to make a better judgement of the likelihood of the other person reciprocating our trust. All these sources of trust exist in

Europe: there has never been more interaction between Europeans—on holidays, in the classroom, in the queue at the supermarket, in your neighbourhood, in the things we eat and drink. These types of interaction might seem banal and mundane, but lie at the very source of how we learn to trust each other.

How is it possible, then, that, despite these sources of trust, so much mistrust exists in Europe? The answer to this seeming contradiction is the European Union. The European Union hasn't been very good at making use of the trust between Europeans. If anything, as we will see in this book, the way in which the EU functions is creating more *dis*trust between citizens than trust. The starting point for the regeneration of Europe, then, will be to rethink how the EU can be changed so that it makes use of the trust between its citizens. Because it is this trust that must be at the core of European integration, and not the internal market, the economic and monetary union, or whichever other policy the European Commission can dream up.

This criticism on the EU's functioning might strike some readers as exaggerated. As we will see in Chap. 4, this ambiguity follows from the fact that the EU has always been very successful. In 1957, when the integration project started, its purpose was to achieve 'peace and prosperity'. Now, more than 60 years later, we can see how incredibly successful the EU has been at achieving these objectives. War between European states seems unthinkable, which, after centuries of almost constant war, is an achievement that cannot be overstated. Poverty still exists in Europe, but, in both absolute and relative terms, the continent has never been more prosperous than today. The secret to the success of the EU has been that its entire set-up, from its institutions to its judicial structure, from the way in which Member States vote down to the way in which law is conceptualised, was constructed with this purpose of 'peace and prosperity' in mind.

Today, however, these objectives no longer seem to inspire much passion in Europe's citizens. The younger generations, who have lived their whole lives in a Europe that is, indeed, peaceful and prosperous, have other worries. They worry about the climate, about debt sustainability, about whether the welfare state will provide them with a pension, about whether they can stay on in a job, and about what effect technological innovations will have on the quality of their lives. All this creates a problem for the EU. Because if the EU wants to stay relevant to its younger generations, it will need to offer them a narrative that engages with the challenges faced by these generations specifically.

To put it as simply as possible, the project of European integration has been remarkably successful at meeting the aspirations of the generations after the war. But if it wants to survive another 60 years, it will need to change tack. Promising peace and prosperity no longer suffice. Nor do the aspirations that the European Commission is currently advertising. At the moment, it seems that the EU is being sold on the basis that it makes roaming slightly cheaper, that it is abolishing daylight savings, and that it protects the privacy of citizens online. This is not to say that these policy initiatives don't have merit; but to say that a project like European integration cannot be sustained by such initiatives. What is needed is a new aspiration for the future of Europe that takes specific account of the challenges and opportunities facing its younger generations. This notion of aspirations is the second big idea that we will look at.

But coming up with a new aspirational framework for the next decades of European integration is only the start of the regeneration of Europe. Because, as we saw, once we have a new aspiration, the only way of *actually achieving it* is by structuring the whole process of European integration—from its institutions to the procedures for voting—in the way that best allows for the achievement of this aspiration. Such revolutionary institutional reforms must be focused around the ability of the European public to engage with the EU. This idea of a public Europe is the third overarching idea in this book and will be discussed in Chap. 5. Rethinking how the EU should institutionally represent Europe is not a job for one man or woman. It should not be Merkel, Macron, Salvini, or Orbán that decides what Europe's new missions should be. It shouldn't be a committee composed of 'wise men', nor a convention of national politicians. It shouldn't be the president of the European Commission, nor should it be me or you. The only way in which the EU will be a stable force in the coming decades is if it internally reorganises itself in a way that is much more sensitive to what European citizens want (from it). The EU must become more accessible, more responsive, and more open to citizens' participation in the decisions that it makes. Only by a willingness to listen to its public can a truly democratic Europe be created.

Strangely, many politicians and academics fear this process. The reason is that opening up the EU and its future to the views of citizens (and politicians from the extreme left and right) would greatly increase conflict and contestation within the EU. To put it simply, it is easy for me to come up with a new vision for the EU, but it is a lot more difficult if I have to convince a majority of Europeans of that vision. Opening up the direction of the European integration process to everyone by making it a *public* question about our *collective* future, then, risks undermining the whole project.

At the same time, as we will see, this is a risk worth taking. Researchers have shown that conflict and contestation are actually quite useful: they engender passion in people, allow them to make links to other citizens that share certain ideas, improve public discussion, increase media (and citizen) awareness of different possible choices, and, ultimately, legitimise the polity. This last part is crucial: it means that more contestation about the future of the EU might actually be a *good* thing for the EU. Why? Because it forces people to be active participants in its construction rather than passive consumers.

The final chapter of the book translates these abstract insights into practice. It suggests ten policy initiatives that could be symbolic of *another* kind of Europe. These initiatives are not meant as 'off the shelf' solutions to the EU's current crisis. They do not serve to fix the EU, but instead offer examples of how the preconditions for *another* Europe could be forged. These proposals range from the whimsical to the wildly ambitious, and have been included regardless of their political feasibility. The point of these ten proposals, rather, is to show what Europe, and the EU, *could* be. If the EU is to survive for another 60 years, it will need to adapt itself to the new challenges that it faces. But it will also need to understand that doing so requires a fundamental transformation, which starts with listening to its younger generations.

CHAPTER 2

The State of Europe

One of the most fundamental changes in western societies over the past decades has been the transformation of the family. Over the past century, the typical family (coined the 'nuclear' family by the anthropologist George Murdoch) has been thought of as a heterosexual couple that lives together, cooperates economically, and raises their own children. That our societies are made up of nuclear families was so straightforward and natural that not many people (or even scholars) had ever imagined other possibilities. More than that, diverting from the norm (e.g. through divorce) was considered a moral failure on the part of the people involved.

All this has changed drastically over the last decades. Since the Netherlands became the first country in the world to permit same-sex marriage, in 2001, 27 other countries have followed suit. Every year more countries recognise same-sex partnership or marriage. Single parenting has almost doubled since 1985. In Denmark, for example, 29% of children aged 0–14 grow up in a household with a single parent. Divorce rates are on the increase in almost every European country despite less and less couples marrying in the first place. New forms of family—composed of a collection of biological and step-parents, composed of parents that do not identify with their biological gender, or formed by use of sperm donors or surrogates—are emerging. This is even without imagining the possible family structures that will emerge once genetic reproductive innovations and sentient artificial intelligence become widely available. What all this indicates is not that the 'idea' of the family is dead, as many conservatives

© The Author(s) 2020
F. de Witte, *re:generation Europe*,
https://doi.org/10.1007/978-3-030-19788-9_2

would have it. What it indicates, instead, is that, at a very basic level, the idea of a *nuclear* family is nothing but a social construction.

A social construction is, in very simple terms, something that exists because many people believe it exists. It is a strange thing, something that is born and dies only by virtue of the collective imagination. Due to their widespread and almost natural acceptance, social constructions are very robust, to the point where they appear impossible to budge. At the same time, social conventions are deeply unstable in cases where their basic premise is challenged. Zeus, Thor, or Indra—the gods that were thought to create thunder and lightning—were a social construction. People believed in them until a better explanation for these natural phenomena emerged. The decline in religious affiliation over the past decades is a result, very simply, of the fact that less and less people believe in an omniscient and omnipotent divine being.

The same goes for the idea of a family. Now that new forms of family are emerging in the west, our understanding of the *nuclear* family is changing because it becomes clear that alternatives *do* exist—that the nuclear family is not necessarily the only (or even the best) way of organising how we live and how we reproduce. The nuclear family, in fact, is a very western and Catholic construction, which fell nicely into step with the demands that early capitalism made on the male workforce. In a sense, the nuclear family can be seen as a historical fluke—a product of very specific historical circumstances. If the modern history of the world between, say, 1600 and 2000 were a simulation, as in the popular computer games such as *Anno, Europa Universalis*, or—for the football fans—*Championship Manager*, the form of family that would emerge in the western world in this period would arguably be different every time the simulation was run. What we think of as constituting a family might be polygamous or consanguine (which revolve around the mother and her bloodline cohabitating, without the father), it could be collective matriarchal families or a system in which grandparents are responsible for bringing up children. We know for a fact that these alternatives to the nuclear family exist for the very simple reason that they have endured in other parts of the world.

Like the family, the European Union is also a social construction. It is something that is constructed by people and survives because people continue to believe in it. It is something that will fail once people stop believing in it. Nation states are the same—even if they are more robustly rooted in historical and cultural narratives. They are the result of random historical circumstances: geography and climate, cultural idiosyncrasies, wars, trade routes, technological innovations, decisions or actions by individual leaders, peace treaties, and large-scale migration. Once again, if we were to run a simulation of the changing political landscape in Europe starting from 1600, the map of Europe today would be different every time that the simulation is run.

And yet, we very seldom think of nation states as existing only because we believe that they, in fact, exist. Scholars call this the idea of 'imagined community': a widely shared belief among citizens that they belong to a 'whole' that is perhaps ill-defined but very tangible in hundreds of daily interactions. And while throughout Europe movements exist that call for secession of regions from already existing states—think of Catalonia or Scotland—no one is seriously arguing that Spain or the United Kingdom ought to stop existing altogether. The argument made, very simply put, is that these regions offer an even stronger version of the 'imagined community' than the nation state can. So why is it that the EU is in an existential crisis, while the nation state is not? Why are nationalism and Euroscepticism on the rise throughout Europe? Is it simply because the EU is too young as a social construction for people to believe in it? Or is there something about the nature of the EU that makes it inherently unstable?

This chapter answers those questions and discusses why the EU is in such a mess—taking account of both political developments and structural problems in the way in which we 'do' European integration. The three most profound and fundamental challenges in the EU's history have all come in the past decade. The Euro-crisis, the refugee crisis, and Brexit all posed a question that seemed irrelevant for 50 years: what is the point of European integration? Is there a point to it in the first place? Do we still believe in it? Or is the EU simply like the gods of thunder—something that we believed in for a while, but that is now outdated?

The Euro-zone crisis, the refugee crisis, and Brexit are all linked to a much more profound transformation of the EU, which has turned an aspirational and progressive project into something that is increasingly met with scepticism and disdain by its citizens. Never has there been more disagreement about what the EU is for; never have there been more internal divisions between the Member States about the future of the project; and never have there been more anti-European, anti-political, and anti-establishment sentiments. This chapter argues that all these processes are linked. It will also argue, however, that social constructions usually survive when they adapt to new circumstances. While the *nuclear* family might be losing ground, this does not mean that the very idea of the family will disappear. Likewise, while the EU might be in a crisis, and might be losing support throughout its Member States, this does not necessarily mean that the very idea of European integration is under threat. If European integration is to survive the next 50 years, however, it will need to adapt to its new environment, the changes in society from 1957 till today, and the new challenges that its citizens face. Before we discuss how to get *out* of the mess that the EU is in today, however, we first need to understand how we got there in the first place.

How to Agree About Money and Refugees?

When philosophers, sociologists, or lawyers talk about social constructions, they are often interested in why these constructions survive. How is it that certain ideas of community or identity such as the nation or race, the image of the nuclear family, monotheism, or democracy endure, while plausible alternatives do not? Part of the answer to this question lies in the way in which people act. By acting in certain ways people, on a daily basis, validate certain social norms. A driver that stops at a pedestrian crossing might not realise it, but in doing so he validates certain symbols (the zebra crossing), certain conventions of cooperation between road users, and the authority of the traffic regulations, police enforcement, and the government that wrote these rules. The strength of social constructions, then, can to some extent be measured by looking at their social acceptability— that is, whether people take them for granted or not. This we all know. Just think of the dramatic swings in public opinion in favour of same-sex marriage over the last decades: once the social acceptance of certain norms disappears, social constructions can change quickly.

Once we move this discussion in the direction of the EU, another term is often used to describe this idea of social acceptability. That is the word *legitimacy*. This word is used to describe whether citizens accept that a certain institution exercises power over them. An illegitimate government is one that has no basis for its power (e.g. because it rules by repression or violence), or one whose norms find no social acceptability. A legitimate government, on the other hand, has come into power through certain fair processes, or where its norms are generally accepted and adhered to by the citizens.

In very general terms, there are two ways for an institutional structure to become legitimate. The first has been called output legitimacy. This is a way of creating social acceptance for government action by creating outcomes or results that are to the liking of the citizens. In simple terms, this creates legitimacy for institutional power by getting certain things done. Institutions whose legitimacy is based on producing certain outputs are often composed of specialists and are insulated from political pressure—think of courts, competition authorities, food or medicine safety agencies or public service provision such as garbage collection, postal services, or water supply. As long as courts are perceived to produce impartial verdicts; competition authorities block abuse of power by big companies; no one dies after buying food or using medicines; garbage is collected; and water and mail arrive when necessary; these institutions survive without problem. Once they no longer achieve their objectives, however, these institutions struggle to maintain their legitimacy. The social acceptance of these institutions, in other words, is primarily tied up with their capacity to *actually* achieve their objectives.

Output legitimacy is central to the way in which the EU functions. The objective of the EU, ever since its origin just after the Second World War, has been to create 'peace and prosperity' on a broken continent. For this, the thinking went, we need experts in charge, and not politicians. It was politicians, after all, that were to blame for the destruction brought on by the war. The central institution of the EU—the European Commission—was therefore deliberately made *un*democratic. It is, indeed, composed of specialists in areas that range from competition policy to climate policy, and from experts in medicines to experts in aviation safety. The legitimacy of the European Commission, and to a large extent the EU as a whole, is, in other words, dependent on it achieving certain results. And it has, in fact, been incredibly successful at achieving these results. The 60-odd years of European integration have brought more peace and prosperity to the EU's Member States than they have ever known before.

At the same time, it is clear that the social acceptance and therefore the legitimacy of the EU are in trouble. More and more political parties on the national level contest the decisions of the EU, and even call in doubt its very existence. Almost every Member State now has its own version—both on the left and on the right—of the *Front National*, the Brexit Party, or *Alternative für Deutschland (AfD)*. What has brought on this shift? Why is the EU under threat if it has been so successful at achieving its objectives?

The answer lies in the basic problem that comes with output legitimacy. It is very difficult for institutions to rely on output legitimacy where alternative answers to a certain question are plausible. Take this example: the two of us walk down an abandoned street and you find three notes of €100. What should we do with it? Should we give it to charity? Should we go for a meal together and spend it? Or should we divide it between us and allow each of us to spend it as they please? And how should we divide it between us, given that you saw the money first? Clearly there is no 'right' answer here—it depends on the intuitions, morals, and personal disposition of the finders. This, in a nutshell, is the problem with institutions that base their legitimacy on achieving certain results or outcomes. The process by which these institutions operate works very well when the result to be achieved is not in dispute. An official of the Commission that is tasked to see if the merger between two companies creates the risk of market distortion will do so using economic models, concepts of market elasticity, or substitutability. Before the European Medicines Agency accepts that a new medicine can be released on the internal market, it has been tested thoroughly in labs, and in randomised and controlled trials. In these cases, institutions derive legitimacy because the outcomes that they are trying to achieve ('prevent abuse of market dominance' or 'no one should die using medicines that are on the market') are not contested. As long as everyone is on board with the objective that is to be achieved, then, institutions can derive sufficient legitimacy by simply achieving those objectives.

The questions that the EU is currently facing, however, do not have an answer that everyone can agree on. Quite the opposite: decisions made in the Euro-zone crisis or the refugee crisis are highly contested within and between Member States. The EU is now acting in areas that deal with the redistribution of money and with questions of identity. These are typically fields in which different answers are possible: should we spend more money on healthcare or education? Should taxation be increased or decreased? Should German banks or Greek pensioners shoulder the burden of the Euro-zone crisis? Should migrants have access to welfare benefits? What should we do with the €300 that we found? Ask these questions to the person sitting next to you, and it is likely that you will disagree with each other about the appropriate answer. Output legitimacy, in these situations, is impossible to achieve simply because there is no agreement on the overall objective that is to be pursued.

Luckily we have the second way of creating social acceptance for institutions, called *input legitimacy*. Input legitimacy is particularly important in answering questions to which there is more than one plausible answer. Let's take the question that is never far from the political debate: whether or not taxes should be raised. Clearly, this question can be answered in many different ways: we may disagree about whether taxes ought to go up or down, we may disagree about which kinds of taxes should be introduced or abolished, and we may disagree about what the added tax revenue should be used for. How can a political institution make a decision about the level of taxation is a way that is considered legitimate by its citizens, that is, in a way that makes citizens accept that decision?

The legitimacy of these types of decision is not dependent on achieving a certain outcome, but is instead dependent on the *process* through which a decision is made. Simply put, input legitimacy is what we often call majoritarian democracy. The legitimacy of a decision to raise taxes, abolish free universities, or be more receptive of refugees comes *solely* from the fact that a majority of citizens think this is the best answer to a certain question. This is a process in which we all participate by voting on a certain political party with a certain party programme. The democratic decision-making process creates legitimacy or social acceptance for decisions because it allows the participation of all citizens, it allows for dissent and contestation, it gives space for all available answers to certain questions, and it leaves policy outcomes open for future reorientation. Even those citizens who have 'lost' in the electoral process accept the outcome, partly because they had a fair shot at 'winning' if only they had convinced more fellow citizens of their view, and partly because they could 'win' in the next electoral cycle. Social acceptability for a certain decision, then, is created where political institutions remain responsive to the views of the citizens.

The EU is not very good at this kind of input legitimacy. The EU is certainly not *un*democratic, as we will see, but it is clearly insufficiently responsive to its citizens in answering questions that have multiple plausible answers. When it comes to money, morals, or values such as community, identity, freedom, or equality, the EU struggles. It even struggles to *ask* these questions: at no point have Europeans ever been asked whether austerity is a good way of 'solving' the Euro-crisis, whether it is a good idea to cut Greek pensions, or whether the repatriation deal with Turkey in order to 'solve' the refugee crisis made sense. The social acceptability of the EU, then, is under threat because it is unable to listen to its citizens when it makes sensitive decisions.

This inability is not accidental—nor is it the fault of the EU. In fact, this inability is a *deliberate* part of how the EU was constructed by the Member States. This makes the often repeated complaint by national politicians that the EU is not sufficiently democratic so hypocritical: it is by deliberate design of the Member States that the EU is not democratic and increasingly struggles to legitimise its decisions. This crucial flaw in the EU's design is, arguably, what connects all the crises that it currently faces: from the Euro-zone crisis to the refugee crisis and Brexit. Underneath the surface of these crises, after all, a much more fundamental question lies: how can the EU offer a legitimate answer to questions on which its 27 Member States disagree?

Caught Between Interdependence ...

The fundamental problem of the EU these days is that it tries to do two things simultaneously that do not go together very well. On the one hand, the EU is making decisions about the challenges facing all the Member States collectively: from the pursuit of economic stability to climate change, from refugee crisis to technological innovations. On the other hand, it is trying to respect national political choices about those very same decisions. Unsurprisingly, the result is a highly complex institutional configuration that is neither particularly efficient nor particularly democratic. It is exactly this uneasy mix between the making of collective decisions and the respect for national choices that is at the source of the rise of the anti-European and anti-establishment parties throughout the EU. But let us start with the more basic question of why the EU struggles to get out of this poisonous position of having to reconcile collective decision-making with respect to national political choices.

One side of the dilemma is the fact that the Member States of the EU are deeply interdependent. This means, essentially, that actions by Member State A have repercussions on Member State B, C, or D. Interdependence, sometimes, is a state of nature. Let's take the Danube as an example. Its source lies in Germany, before flowing 2888 kilometres through Austria, Slovakia, Hungary, Croatia, Serbia, Bulgaria, and Romania. If Germany allows its industries to dump highly toxic waste in the Danube, it will severely affect the capacity of Hungary or Bulgaria to use the Danube for drinking water or to allow it as a site for recreation. Likewise, if Austria decides to build a massive dam in the river to generate power, secure drinking water, and irrigate the whole country; this will have an impact on the capacity of Romania to do exactly the same. The other evident example of interdependence, of course, is the battle against climate change. It is abundantly clear that Belgium or Ireland have very little capacity to reverse global warming if they act on their own: they are dependent on the cooperation of other states.

Sometimes, however, interdependence is not a state of nature, but is instead deliberately created. One of the objectives of the European integration project, in fact, was to create such a deep level of interdependence between nation states that war became a practical impossibility. Starting a war against a neighbouring state on which you depend for access to food, energy, or economic stability, the logic went, would be such an egregious act of self-harm that states no longer have the incentive to fight. Sixty-odd years on, the process of European integration has made the Member States interdependent not only in an economic sense—through the creation of an internal market with free movement of factors of production—but also in monetary policy, migration policy, in relation to family law, tax law, and welfare law. There are, in fact, very few decisions that Member States make that do *not* have a potential impact on their neighbouring states.

Let me offer some scenarios to drive this point home. Imagine that Spain, overwhelmed by the plight of desperate refugees risking their lives crossing the Mediterranean, decides that the only possible response is to open its borders in Ceuta and Melilla, so that these refugees can have safe passage into Spanish territory. These refugees and migrants can then, however, take the ferry to Algeciras and travel freely throughout the EU— given the absence of physical borders in the Schengen area. This means that Finland, Poland, or Austria might be faced with a surge in refugees due to a decision that falls outside of their control. A democratically mandated decision by the Spanish parliament, in other words, has an effect on its neighbouring Member States, which have had no say in the Spanish decision to open its borders. Now let's imagine that, faced with the high numbers of refugees, Italy, Germany, and Belgium decide to close their borders—again, after a democratic decision by their national parliaments. This might mean that thousands of refugees are stuck in France—unable to proceed to other Member States. Again, this means that the democratic decision of one state (Italy) has an effect on its neighbouring state (France). I could extend this example indefinitely—but the point is clear: in situations of interdependence, it is problematic if we allow Member States to make their own decisions without regard for the effects that these decisions have on their neighbouring states.

The same logic applies to decisions of Member States that are interdependent due to their membership of the Euro. Given that the Euro-zone is managed through a single monetary policy by the European Central

Bank, Member States are not allowed to make certain decisions in taxation or welfare spending that might upset the overall stability of the Euro. This was borne out dramatically, of course, in the discussions on Greek debt repayment. In return for financial aid, Greece has had to comply with a range of public sector cuts, including state pensions, funding for health-care, the privatisation of public services, and the increase of specific taxa-tion regimes. The logic here, once again, is one of interdependence: if Greece were allowed to make its own democratic decisions (e.g., *not* to cut healthcare spending to a level unprecedented in any other Member State), this would have a negative effect on the *other* Member States.

The interdependence between the EU's Member States suggests that decisions that affect multiple Member States—such as what happens to the Danube, the conditions for entry into the Schengen area, the rules of public spending for Euro-zone countries, or the rules on arresting crimi-nals, recognising divorces, or quality controls on foods—should be made together. Only by making these decisions together, after all, are the inter-ests and views of *all* the Member States (and their citizens) that are affected by the decisions taken into account.

... AND INDEPENDENCE

If one part of the EU's fundamental dilemma is the fact that its Member States are interdependent in almost every policy area; the other part of the dilemma is that the EU is, at the same time, deeply committed to the independence or autonomy of its Member States. This makes for a very impractical combination. The EU's commitment to the independence of its Member States comes, simply put, from the fact that without Member States there can be no EU—as Brexit shows. The EU *must* be sensitive to the feelings and democratic decisions of its Member States to ensure that it can survive. This central role for Member States can be seen in the EU's institutions, where no law can be made unless it is agreed by the ministers of the Member States, by the fact that EU Treaties can only be changed if *all* Member States and all national parliaments agree, and by the commit-ment in the Treaty to respect the constitutional identities of the Member States.

What underlies this commitment to protect the independence of the Member States is, once again, the need for the EU to be legitimate. As we saw in the previous section, the EU is very good at generating output legitimacy, but struggles to secure input legitimacy. In other words, it is not very good at being responsive to the citizens' assessment of how certain sensitive policy questions should be answered. The EU's solution to this legitimacy problem has been quite simple: it *borrows* input legitimacy from its Member States. What the EU is weakest at—collecting individual opinions of its citizens, discussing available policy alternatives, engendering media attention and citizens' awareness about the possible choices, and ensuring that the eventual outcome corresponds to the majority view—is exactly what the Member States are very good at.

The democratic machinery that creates input legitimacy on the national level is very sophisticated—and has developed, in many Member States, over at least 100 years. It consists not just of political parties that are integrated from the municipal level all the way up to the national parliament but also of grass-root movements, activists, expert bureaucracies, and a whole support cast of media outlets that ensure that citizens discuss the same problems with each other. This sophisticated institutional machinery is indispensible in ensuring that citizens are listened to, have a chance to shape the society in which they live, and that politicians can respond to new problems that they are faced with. The big trump card of democracy, in fact, is that it cannot resist listening: as soon as a certain opinion is held by a sufficiently large group of citizens, a politician will almost automatically emerge that represents that opinion.

The EU's need to borrow legitimacy from the national level is the reason why it remains so strongly committed to the autonomy of its Member States. Sensitive decisions, such as dealing with the distribution of money or opportunities in society, with morality, or with notions of identity, equality, or community, can only legitimately be decided through a process that listens to the citizens that are affected by those decisions.

The problem with this approach, however, is that people disagree about how these questions should be answered. Just as you and I might disagree about what to do with the €300 that we find in an abandoned street, Member States differ on how questions relating to Greek debt repayment, the hosting of Syrian refugees, or a new free-trade deal with the United States should be answered. Member States, simply put, come up with different answers to the same question.

Where the interdependence between Member States and the independence of those Member States clash, then, we have a problem. Something has to give. Either we allow Member States to make their own decisions, regardless of the costs that they create for each other, or we come up with a *single* answer for all the Member States, regardless of the fact that it might be against the democratic wishes of certain countries.

The perfect example of this problem was the dramatic European Council in the summer of 2015, when Greece barely avoided being pushed out of the Euro-zone. The setting was a perfect storm of interdependence and independence. Alexis Tsipras, the Greek Prime Minister, had just secured a comfortable win in a referendum that rejected the austerity terms that were imposed on Greece in return for a new credit line. His democratic mandate, in other words, was to say 'no' to austerity. The democratic mandate of Merkel, however, was exactly the opposite: she had campaigned on a platform of ensuring that German taxpayers' money would only go to Greece in return for significant austerity measures. Given the interdependence between Germany and Greece, both tied to a *single* currency and monetary policy, however, it was clear that it is impossible to simultaneously have austerity *and* have no austerity.

What happens in these circumstances is that one of the two sides wins, and with it, one of the two domestic political mandates. The result of the Greek referendum, in which the Greek population clearly and overwhelmingly voted *against* further austerity measures, proved utterly meaningless. The consequence is that the legitimacy of the EU is further weakened: the EU is increasingly seen as an institution that does not respect the wishes of (some parts of) its citizenry and that prevents citizens from being able to control the way in which their society operates. As we saw, this is dangerous territory: without sufficient legitimacy for the decisions that it takes, the social acceptance of the EU gradually weakens.

This dilemma between independence and interdependence of European states cannot be resolved without fundamentally changing the way in which we 'do' European integration. At the same time, it is also the dilemma that lies at the centre of the remarkable emergence of anti-European and anti-establishment parties throughout the EU.

The Problem with Democracy in Europe

The problem with democracy in Europe is that we have created an almost perfect mismatch between the level where we answer political questions and the level where we discuss what these answers should be. On the national level, as we saw, we have a sophisticated machinery that is equipped to ensure that the citizens' opinions are channelled into politics, and mechanisms that ensure that politicians are punished when they do not fulfil their mandates. Yet, less and less questions can still be answered on the national level, because allowing for this would create significant costs for neighbouring states.

On the European level, on the other hand, where decisions that affect all Member States must be taken so that all interests can be taken into account, we lack almost all preconditions for a functioning democracy. There are no transnational political parties that try to win our vote, no conflicting mandates between parties that clarify different available options for the citizen, no heavily mediatised electoral cycle, hardly any media coverage of legislative action, no transnational media that binds the electorate, no capacity for citizens to control the legislative agenda, and no possibility for citizens to punish politicians when they do not meet their promises. This leads, simply put, to the fact that it is very difficult to directly legitimise decisions taken on the European level.

The EU's tactic to manage this mismatch has been to ensure that Member States have a *legal* obligation to respect certain policy rules in areas in which they are mutually interdependent. These rules are often written down in the Treaty, which means that it is practically impossible to change the rules of the game (short of agreement between *all* the Member States *and* their parliaments). The content of these rules range from a commitment to the internal market, free movement of factors of production, equal treatment of European citizens, certain democratic values, a commitment to price stability, and a ban on state aid for domestic industries. Beyond these basic rules, collective decisions are made by what is called 'qualified majority voting', which means that Member States can protect their own interests, but can also be outvoted if a large majority of the other Member States and their citizens disagree with a certain position.

Arguably, it is this tactic of managing the process of integration that is at the root of the anti-European and anti-establishment populism. Whether in the form of Le Pen or Mélenchon, Orbán, Kaczyński, Salvini, or Grillo, in the guise of *the Brexit Party, AfD, Forum voor Democratie,* or the *True Finns,* one thing is clear: the voters are disillusioned with the EU, the political centre, and the political elite. The EU is, arguably, at least partly to blame for this. Brexit probably offers the best way to explain this logic. Analysis of electoral data after the Brexit referendum shows a clear cleavage between a group of citizens that fare well under conditions of global competition and global opportunities, and those who feel that they have lost out because of the process of globalisation—be it economically, socially, or culturally. This new dividing line in politics, between 'internationalists' and 'nativists', was largely mirrored in the French and US presidential elections that took place in the year after the Brexit referendum, and has been a prominent theme in elections throughout the EU ever since—from Austria to Italy and from Poland to Sweden.

The emergence of this new dividing line is a result (at least partially) of the way in which the EU operates. In the EU, the commitment to 'internationalism', in the form of the free movement of factors of production, citizens, and austerity, has been entrenched in the Treaty and in the EU's legal system. That means that it *cannot* be altered without the unanimous consent of 27 governments, their parliaments, *and* their electorates. To put this point as starkly as possible, a 50.1% majority of Maltese parliament (representing 215,000 Europeans) can resist *any* change to this commitment to internationalism even if all other Member States (representing over 500,000,000 Europeans) are in favour. Given that there will always be Member States that benefit from the EU's commitment to internationalism, this makes it close to impossible to change the basic socio-economic contract that underlies the EU. The EU's tactic of managing the interdependence between the Member States, in other words, *is exactly the reason* why certain political questions have been lifted outside the realm of political contestation.

What makes the situation in the EU even more problematic is that the EU's commitment to internationalism cannot be contested on the national level, either. Given the incapacity of *one* single government to change anything about this commitment, national political parties have a clear incentive to support internationalism. After all, if they promise to change, say, the migration rules for workers coming from other Member States, state aid rules to allow for big government investments in certain sectors of the economy, or the rules for expulsion of non-EU migrants—they will quickly realise that these promises are impossible to maintain without support of *all other* Member States. As Tsipras realised after the European Council in 2015, even an explicit mandate in the form of a national referendum was not sufficient to change the EU's commitment to austerity. Equally, Salvini's promise of expelling 500,000 non-EU migrants from Italy is impossible to maintain without violating EU obligations, or convincing all other Member States to change the rules. This means that certain views of society are simply set in stone in Europe, and that alternative visions are unavailable. Again, it is important to highlight that this was—and still is— a deliberate part of the EU's construction, not a fluke. As Donald Tusk, the president of the European Council, argued in 2015, in the aftermath of Tsipras' rebellion: 'this new intellectual mood, my intuition is it's risky for Europe. Especially this radical leftish illusion that you can build some alternative to this traditional European vision of society.'[1] The way in which the EU is managing the clash between interdependence and independence, then, is by simply removing some political questions off the table.

The result of this has been a thorough depoliticisation of the EU's and Member States' commitment to internationalism. Mainstream political parties have simply stopped to argue about this commitment. It is not politically wise to promise something that cannot be delivered, after all. And so, even if the traditional centre-left parties throughout the EU are uncomfortable with the liberal premises of the internal market; and even if the traditional centre-right parties tend to disagree with the rules on free movement of persons; neither has meaningfully contested these core principles of the EU's social contract for decades. Parties on the extreme left and right, on the other hand, have a much easier sell. Whether it is Mélenchon or Le Pen, their premise is simple: *only* by leaving the EU will we be able to control economic policy or migration policy in a way that is sensitive to what our national citizens want from it. In other words, the lack of space for political contestation *within* the EU has caused a reaction from national voters: they start to contest the EU *as such*.

This political narrative of questioning membership to the EU in order to allow national citizens to *take back control* over its money, borders, environmental or social policy is clearly successful. The irony, of course, as Brexit shows, is that the economic and regulatory interdependence between nation states in twenty-first-century Europe is such that a meaningful reappropriation of control is impossible. That does not mean, however, that the narrative is wrong, or that voters have somehow been misled. It shows that the EU must ensure that citizens feel that they can control and alter the basic socio-economic conditions under which they live their lives. It also shows, more ominously for the EU, that national contestation of a certain policy area of the EU (whether these are the rules on migration, monetary policy, healthcare, or state aid) can easily spill over into contestation of the EU *as such*. In the simplest possible terms, the EU must allow more control for its citizens in order to protect its own legitimacy and ensure its survival.

All this leads to a vicious circle that consists of four steps:

(i) The only way in which we can effectively manage the ties of interdependence between Member States that exist because of the internal market, the borderless Schengen area, the monetary system, and external circumstances such as the war in Syria, is by making collective decisions on the European level. Only by making decisions on the European level that constrain *alternative decisions* by Member States do we prevent national choices from creating externalities, or negative consequences, for a nation's neighbouring states. However, on the European level we lack a mechanism of making sure that we answer divisive choices in a way that correspond to the citizens' wishes. The solution to this conundrum has been to 'borrow' national mandates for European decisions. In other words, citizens discuss 'at home' what they think the appropriate solution to the Euro-crisis or refugee crisis should be and appoint politicians based on those discussions, who are then sent to Brussels to fulfil their mandate. Except that, of course, these 27 national mandates tend to conflict and cannot be met simultaneously.

(ii) In consequence, national voters tend to feel betrayed by their own politicians and fail to understand why 'Brussels' takes a certain decision. Once a decision has been taken by 'Brussels', however, it is almost impossible to reverse. This applies not just to policy decisions, but also to certain rules that have been laid down in the Treaty (such as rules on free movement, market freedom, state aid, or monetary policy). All this leads to a situation in which certain promises can no longer be made by national politicians—because they know fully well that they cannot convince fellow Member States to support them—or, worse, *are* made by national politicians who subsequently blame 'Brussels' (even though their main interlocutors are the other Member States rather than the European institutions) when they cannot be delivered. This process has alienated the voters from the political elites on the national and European level.

(iii) It has also led to something that can be called 'extreme centrism', whereby the traditional political families throughout Europe—typically the social-democrats, Christian-democrats, and the liberals—have stopped contesting each other on many issues of the socio-economic structures that define our lives. After all, what point is there to promise anything other than the socio-economic contract that all Member States are forced to follow? For many voters, the mainstream political parties have become virtually indistinguishable over the past decades. These parties have not only 'lost touch' with their voters, but also struggle to translate new discontent into political agendas, wherever such discontent requires changing the EU's social contract. This process has created the space in the political spectrum for anti-establishment and anti-European parties to emerge on the fringes of the left and right. These parties promise more national control over the conditions under which we all live, and are increasingly contesting the very existence of the EU as the *one* thing that stands in their way.

(iv) As a result, Member States are becoming more nationalist, either because nativist parties are in power or because centrist parties feel that they must respond to the nativists in order to cling on to power. This process makes cooperating within the context of the EU even more difficult: how can we solve a certain problem that we face together (whether it is the refugee crisis, the Euro-zone crisis, or climate change) in a political climate wherein national interests and national choices must be defended at all costs? The answer is simple: it is impossible. Which brings us to a crossroad: either we come up with a solution to our collective problems that doesn't necessarily respect the national choices of *all* Member States, in which case we go back to point (i), or we end up at a point where the EU simply loses so much of its legitimacy—or social acceptability among the citizens—that it ceases to exist.

This vicious circle suggests that while the way in which we 'do' European integration might have been the best way in 1957, it is no longer the best way today. In fact, the EU's current tactic for managing interdependence is undermining the belief that people have in the EU. The emergence of Euroscepticism, anti-establishment parties, and resurgent nationalism is at least partially caused by the fundamental mismatch between the level at which we take decisions in the EU (in Brussels) and the level at which we decide what those decisions should look like (in national capitals). This challenge to the way in which we 'do' integration is arguably an even more serious problem for the EU than the Euro-crisis, the refugee crisis, or Brexit put together. After all, it questions the very premise on which the EU is based: why are we even cooperating in the first place?

Visions of the Future: The EU or the Nation State?

What will the political map of Europe look like in 50 years? Will the boundaries of the nation states have remained the same? Will the EU still exist—will it be a federation of regions, a fully-fledged state, or have become an outdated symbol of a certain period in Europe's history? Today these questions might seem far-fetched. And yet, things change. If history tells us something, it is that borders between nations continuously shift, emerge, and disappear. Especially in times of crisis, moreover, strange things can happen very quickly. As we saw in the introduction to this chapter, the nation state and the EU are social constructions. They only exist (and survive) because we—collectively—believe they do exist and should exist. Once these basic foundations become weaker, for example, by people questioning the merit or value of a certain organisation, social constructions can change beyond recognition very quickly.

And so it is perhaps prudent, in the moment of the EU's deepest crisis since its inception, to think about what could come next. There are two obvious answers to this question. One is to go backwards, towards a Europe in which the nation state has full control over what happens within its borders. The other option is to go forward, to have 'more Europe', and to accept that the EU plays a crucial part in managing the territories and citizens of all its Member States. Both answers, as is often the case with obvious answers, are problematic for different reasons.

The option to increase the power of the nation states in the EU is one that has gained traction throughout the Member States. Brexit, of course, is a perfect example of this process: it is the reassertion of national control over the rules that are in force on its territory and that bind its citizens. From Brexit day onwards, the thinking goes, the United Kingdom will regain its sovereignty to make its own decisions when it comes to the rules of the market, the rules on migration, fisheries, the environment, data privacy, and competition law. An alternative version of this vision for the future of Europe is the one espoused by Marine Le Pen, Geert Wilders, and Matteo Salvini. They are not necessarily against European integration as such, but are very suspicious of the EU—that is, the current incarnation of European integration. In their view, cooperation between independent and autonomous nation states should take place with retention of the power of states to make their own decisions. In Le Pen's own words in an interview with *Der Spiegel*: 'I want to destroy the EU, not Europe! I believe in a Europe of nation-states. I believe in Airbus and Ariane, in a Europe based on cooperation. But I don't want this European Soviet Union.'[2] This vision of the future of the EU—whereby cooperation is limited to making decisions that everyone can agree on—is very much based on the sentiment that the EU is not sufficiently responsive to its citizens and respectful of the differences between them.

The problem with this approach is that it is based on the fallacy that a nation state is able to control the conditions under which their citizens live. The explicit objective of this 'nativist' vision of the future of Europe is to ensure that sensitive decisions (such as those relating to money, morals, identity, culture, or migration) can be made, altered, and controlled by the national electorate *alone*. The problem, of course, is that increasing the political control of national actors has the important side effect of *decreasing* the capacity of a neighbouring state to do exactly the same! A Hungarian decision that prevents the entry of refugees *does* have an effect on its neighbouring states; a rejection by the Greek population of certain effects of austerity *does* have an effect on the other Member States and citizens in the Euro-zone; and Italy refusing entry to its ports to a ship carrying hundreds of migrants *does* have an effect on Malta, Spain, or France. As long as nation states in Europe are interdependent, strengthening nation state powers is likely to lead to *less* rather than more control for national citizens. It also risks creating antagonism between nation states, which was, of course, the very problem that European integration sought to resolve.

To this criticism, a 'nativist' might say: we should abolish the Euro and Schengen, and thereby weaken the interdependence between nation states in Europe. Brexit, however, shows that this does not make much of a difference. The United Kingdom has never been part of Schengen or the Euro-zone. And yet, it seems that much of the illusory control that the Brexiteers were seeking to 'take back', will, in fact, not come back to Westminster. In economic terms, every European nation state needs access to the common market—the biggest in the world in terms of GDP. In security terms, every European nation state is keen to share information and enforcement capacities to thwart terrorist attacks or apprehend criminals across borders. In terms of global politics, all European states need to speak with one voice to have a remote change of engaging the global superpowers on topics ranging from trade, nuclear disarmament, or climate change. The United Kingdom—even after Brexit—will be tied to

European rules on issues that range from residence rights for citizens, regulatory standards on products, environment and taxation, norms on data sharing, and rules on surveillance and police cooperation. The only meaningful difference is that the United Kingdom will not be part of the Member States making those rules.

This is simply by virtue of the fact that the reality of the twenty-first century is that nation states *are* interdependent if they want to meet their electorate's expectations. Short of stopping technological innovations, blocking internet access, and rescaling domestic industries to be fully self-sufficient in the production of food, energy, products, and services; interdependence is simply here to stay. And with interdependence, inescapably, comes a choice: either cooperation with the possible loss of control over all policy preferences, or *no* cooperation with the risk of having certain policy choices imposed on you.

The problem with the 'nativist' vision of the future of Europe, then, is that it doesn't really take the citizen very seriously. It is a knee-jerk reaction that offers an illusion of control without realising that national control in nation state A might have negative repercussions for that same control of the citizens of nation state B. It fails to take seriously the point that—ultimately—the only legitimate fashion of government is where all citizens can equally control the conditions under which they collectively live their lives.

The second obvious vision for the future of the EU is the opposite: it is not one that suggests 'less' but 'more' Europe. It is one that suggests that the issues that all Europeans face together—from economic stagnation to migration from the Middle East and Africa, from climate change to reforms of the welfare state—can only be solved by giving power to Brussels rather than to national capitals. What matters more than anything to proponents of this view is *getting things done*, that is, achieving results. While there are many forms of this vision of 'more Europe', the most recent and explicit has been the position of the French President Emmanuel Macron. In a series of speeches in the years following his election, he laid down a vision for the future of the EU in which more and more powers move from the national capitals to the EU.

His vision is based on two pillars. On the one hand, the EU should 'do more' in order to achieve its objectives, such as economic stability, refugee protection, and climate change. Macron has suggested, for example, the establishment of a system of carbon tax, digital taxation, of European funds disbursed to communities willing to take in refugees, a Euro-zone budget made up out of corporate taxation, the creation of 'genuine' European universities, and a European agency for disruptive innovation. On the other hand, the European institutions should gradually become more democratic—such as through the creation of a new European Parliament specific to the Euro-zone, or the creation of a European Finance Ministry. Macron's vision, then, is to do more things in Brussels, and to bolster the legitimacy of EU action by enhancing the democratic elements of the way in which it is governed.

While many of Macron's ideas have great merit (the latter parts of this book, in fact, will support some of them), the problem with his approach is that he struggles to cede control of the direction of travel of European integration. Macron's approach, in a sense, is simply to enter in a new destination in the *satnav* that steers the course of European integration. This is not what democracy is about, however. Democracy is about letting the citizens steer the car. The purpose of Macron's vision of democratisation is not to offer the steering wheel to the European citizens, but is to ensure a smoother ride towards the destination that *he* has entered in the *satnav*. His proposals for a Euro-zone Parliament, for example, serve to legitimise the creation of a transfer union based on collection of corporate taxation, and disbursed under conditions set by the Member States. It is *not* a forum where citizens can answer the policy question: do we want austerity or not? Where should taxation come from and how should we use it?

The future of the EU, under Macron, is still based on a functional bias: it serves to achieve very specific and already agreed outcomes. As we saw earlier, however, if it is impossible to challenge these outcomes, we cannot meaningfully speak of democracy. As the German political scientist Fritz Scharpf has put it: 'politicisation without the possibility of autonomous policy choices is more likely to produce frustration, alienation, apathy or rebellion rather than democratic legitimation.'[3] The problem with Macron's (and others') vision of 'more Europe', then, is that it struggles to open up the process of integration to the wishes and needs of its citizenry. The need to agree on functional objectives that the integration process should obtain is so entrenched that it has almost become impossible—even to the most ardent pro-Europeans, like Macron—to envision a future of the EU that is actually in the hands of its citizens.

CONCLUSION

This chapter has identified the challenges that the EU currently faces. Underneath the ones that are visible on the surface—Brexit, the Eurozone crisis, and the refugee crisis—there is a deeper challenge for the EU. It must come to grips with the question of how to make collective decisions in situations where Member States disagree. Without an answer to this question, the legitimacy of the EU will keep taking hits. Big steps forward—towards 'more Europe'—or backwards—towards nation state control—are not capable of allowing citizens to understand and control the conditions under which they live their lives. And without this control, it is only a matter of time before the existential question is asked: is the EU still worth it? And if not, is another institutional vision of Europe more appealing or more plausible?

The rest of the book will argue that a third choice is possible—beyond a step backward or forward. It will argue that it is time to give up on the understanding of European integration as we have until now. Just as the nuclear family was a fluke of history—a product of an odd mix of Catholicism, colonial expansion, and early capitalism—and is now being reconfigured to accommodate changes in cultural and moral sensitivities, visions of personhood, and economic realities, so the EU must change. This is not a question of giving up on European integration—quite the opposite. Only by fundamentally rethinking how and why we should 'do' Europe can it possibly be saved.

The two starting points for the argument in this book are the following. First, we must take account of the Europe that already exists: a Europe that links Arctic landscapes with Greek temples; the legend of count Dracula with that of Jeanne d'Arc; and that links a pint of Guinness with a *pizza margherita*. Europe is, at its most basic, an unparalleled range of foods, cultures, habits, and geographies. This is not something to resist, but something to celebrate. Second, we must adapt the EU to the realities of today. The younger generations of Europeans—whose support for the EU will be indispensible if it is to survive—face very different challenges than the ones that the EU was constructed to face. Only by understanding what it is that those generations want from the EU can the EU secure the support of these groups of citizens. The following chapters will describe what the EU could look like if it is to be more sensitive to its own diversity, more sensitive to what its younger generations want from it, and willing to offer the steering wheel of the process of integration to its citizens.

NOTES

1. Financial Times, 17th July 2015, '*Donald Tusk interview: the annotated transcript*'.
2. Der Spiegel, 3rd June 2014, '*Interview with Marine Le Pen: "I don't want this Soviet European Union".*'
3. F. Scharpf, *After the Crash. A Perspective on Multilevel European Democracy* (2015) 21 European Law Journal 398.

CHAPTER 3

Trust

In 1998 Patrick La Prairie, a journalist for the French newspaper *Ouest-France*, woke up with an idea. He was in charge of the newspaper's outreach to school children and had come up with a project that would engage school kids with the European integration project. The idea was deceptively simple: even though the EU had adopted—from the Council of Europe—its flag, it did not have a motto. There was no equivalent to the French *liberté, égalité, fraternité* to signify what the EU stood for. La Prairie's idea was to let European school kids come up with a motto, as a light-hearted and low-threshold way of getting them to think about what the EU is and what it stands for.

After having found some sponsors, and having agreed on a cooperation with newspapers in the other Member States (including *The Guardian*, *La Repubblica*, and *Berliner Zeitung*), La Prairie managed to involve around 80,000 school kids in coming up with a new motto for the EU. From each of the (then) 15 Member States a winner was selected, and the classes that had won the national rounds were all invited to Brussels, where the final winner was picked by an eclectic bunch of Europeans—ranging from a Belgian astronaut to Jacques Delors, a former president of the European Commission. The jury commended the mottos *'peace, freedom and solidarity'*; *'united for peace and democracy!'*; *'an old continent, a new hope'*; and *'all different, all Europeans!'* before announcing that a class from Luxembourg had carried the day. The winning motto was *'unity in diversity'*—and was adopted in a slightly different version (*'united in diversity'*)

© The Author(s) 2020
F. de Witte, *re:generation Europe*,
https://doi.org/10.1007/978-3-030-19788-9_3

as the official motto of the EU a year later. One of the jury members, the former Austrian chancellor Franz Vranitzky, noted that 'the reference to diversity evokes the wind. A sailing boat goes downwind, but, with a good crew, it also progresses in headwind.'[1]

This chapter discusses something that the Luxembourg school kids realised but escaped the attention of the former Austrian chancellor. For him, as for many leaders of the EU throughout its history, diversity is like headwind—something that makes cooperation, or progress, much more difficult if not impossible. The EU's *ethos*, its guiding logic, is indeed one that understands diversity as something that must be overcome. This guiding logic is born out of a fear that differences between Member States and their citizens would lead to antagonism, war, and thereby prevent cooperation. Ensuring a level of uniformity across Europe by decreasing its diversity, the thinking went, would lead to familiarity between Europeans and thereby strengthen the trust between them, which, in turn, would make it easier for them to cooperate. And to a large extent, that is what the EU has been doing for the past 60 years. Whether you live in Krakow or Seville, the EU sets exactly the same rules that regulate the composition of your breakfast cereal, the quality of your make-up, dictate your privacy settings on Facebook, set roaming charges, and deal with the safety of your children's toys.

The depressing element in this story is that the EU's strategy seems to be backfiring. The life of someone in Krakow and someone in Seville may have never been more similar, and yet, the distrust between Europeans has never been higher since 1957. Despite less and less headwind, the sailing boat of European integration is struggling to advance. Even more depressing is that the EU is clearly missing a trick—something that the Luxembourg school kids intuitively understood. What the EU thinks of as its main weakness—the immense diversity among Europeans—could easily be turned into its main strength. Because if Europe has one strength, it is its diversity. Think about pretty much any topic, and you will find an extravagant diversity throughout Europe: from climate to fashion; from landscapes to TV-shows; from languages and food to art and architecture; from general predisposition to humour; from breakfast routines and school marking systems to history and social conventions. Nowhere in the world is there such a concentration of wonderful and gloriously diverse cultural and social practices. Why would anyone—let alone the EU, which is meant to be the institutional echo of Europe—want to decrease this?

This is especially so since, as we will see, trust is more likely to emerge by *celebrating* diversity than by destroying it.

This chapter will argue why the EU's pursuit of uniformity and centralisation should be resisted—and *can* be resisted without decreasing trust between European citizens and without making cooperation between them more difficult. Any project of regeneration of Europe must start, in fact, by building on the trust that already exists between its citizens. This chapter will show that *despite* the differences between Europeans, trust among them is in plentiful supply, and will likely increase in the coming decades. The real question is how the EU can make sure that it captures and co-opts this trust in a way that is more sensitive to what Europe really is: a wonderfully diverse continent.

DIVERSITY AND EUROPEAN INTEGRATION

Until I was six years old, I lived in Italy with my parents. My classmates and I were told that if we had been 'good' during the whole year, *La Befana*—a witch flying through the night sky on a broomstick—would fill our socks with candy and presents on the night of 6th January. When we moved to the Netherlands, however, I was told a different story. In the Netherlands, kids are rewarded for having been 'good' by *Sinterklaas*—an old man that comes from Spain on his boat and travels the Dutch rooftops on a white horse—on the night of 5th December. My parents got out of the obvious confusion that followed by insisting that both *La Befana* and *Sinterklaas* are part of an eclectic group of characters that take care of 'good' boys and girls and had simply split up their respective territories for reasons of efficiency.

A few years later I saw this confusion reflected in the friends that I played football with. In the Netherlands, football highlights are broadcast on Sunday evening in a TV-show called *Studio Sport*. The first game that is shown is the most important and eagerly anticipated match of the weekend, and we would go out of our way not to know the results before watching the show. As my friends started sharing my passion for Italian football, they would come over to watch the Italian equivalent—a show called *90° minuto*. To their surprise (and dismay), *90° minuto starts* by giving away the results of all the matches, and then proceeds to show the most boring match of the weekend first, before ending the show with the most exciting matches. My friends cannot—even today—understand why anyone would want to spoil the pleasure of watching highlights by announcing the results beforehand.

Europeans experience these mild and amusing feelings of disorientation and shock on a daily basis—whether on holiday or in observing their neighbours, classmates, or colleagues that come from another country. The differences between Europeans cover every aspect of daily life: how children are raised, what behaviour is acceptable in restaurants, how we shop or celebrate good news, how we spend summer, or what transport we use.

All these differences are often considered a problem for European integration. How can we, after all, cooperate and learn to trust each other if we are *so* different?

Differences in the way European states organise themselves are, indeed, the most basic problem for many of the policy areas of the EU: from the regulation of the internal market and the management of the Euro-zone to environmental policy and the rules on migration. Let's take an example to drive this point home. Imagine that in Spain only green shampoo can be sold in the supermarkets. Imagine that in Portugal only red shampoo can be sold. This—admittedly simplistic—example demonstrates the problem that the EU faces in a million different ways: how to foster cooperation between Member States that are *so* different in everything they do? How can we all cooperate in *one* internal market when Portuguese and Spanish consumers differ so clearly in the way they 'do' things? How can we ever be united if the headwind of diversity is so strong?

One answer is to harmonise standards. This means setting a collective, EU-wide standard on the colour of shampoo that can be sold. What this standard ends up being does not matter: Spanish and Portuguese producers and consumers will be bound by the same rules, and, over time, familiarity will breed trust. The logic of harmonisation, in other words, is one whereby uniformity is often seen as a *prerequisite* for cooperation. If consumers throughout Europe know that they can buy the same or similar shampoo, trousers, cucumbers, and light bulbs whether in Varna, Porto, or Rennes, they will no longer care if the product is produced in Helsinki, Zagreb, or Maastricht. The same logic applies to the management of the Euro-zone or of Schengen: if all Member States agree to abide by the same rules, there is no reason anymore to distrust each other. This method of generating trust between Member States that are very different, however, comes at a cost. Harmonisation is obviously not a very good way of respecting local differences or traditions.

The EU has therefore come up with another solution for allowing cooperation and trust *despite* differences between Member States. This solution is called the principle of mutual recognition or mutual trust. Simply put, these principles get round the problem of difference by pretending it doesn't exist. As you can imagine, this isn't exactly the most sustainable strategy. These principles oblige Member States to treat foreign products, workers, or even criminals *as if they were nationals.* This probably sounds a bit counterintuitive. In practice it means that a cucumber grown in Spain can be sold in Finland *even though* it does not meet the standards for cucumber production in Finland. Finland must *trust* that Spanish regulations on the production of cucumbers protect their consumers in a similar fashion as their own rules. The same goes for a Belgian engineer, who can build a bridge in Slovenia without meeting the qualification condition set for Slovenian engineers. The Slovenian authorities must trust that Belgian universities prepare an engineer sufficiently well for the job. Finally, the same goes for Irish authorities that are asked to arrest a Polish criminal for crimes he did not commit in Ireland. Ireland must trust that the arrest warrant is genuine and that the criminal will receive a fair trial when extradited to Poland.

The logic underlying mutual recognition and mutual trust is that, while Member States may regulate things differently, they often try to achieve the *same* objective—whether it is the protection of the health of consumers of cucumber, the quality of higher education, or that criminals are caught and prosecuted. Mutual recognition and mutual trust, then, are quite elegant mechanisms to ensure that Member States can work together notwithstanding the differences between them. It allows the EU to achieve its objectives without having to bulldoze differences between how things are done in different parts of Europe. The rules on mutual recognition, then, are, to use the analogy of the former Austrian chancellor, the crew of the sailing boat of integration that allows for progress despite the headwind of diversity.

While mutual recognition and mutual trust may sound great on paper, however, it seems that these concepts have a sort of accidental bulldozing property of their own. Over the past years alone, the European Court of Justice has argued that the following rules—that essentially reflect differences in the way society is organised in different countries—have to be scrapped because they don't respect the rights of cross-border traders: Germany's rules protecting rural pharmacies, Dutch and Spanish rules protecting the liveability of small cities by pushing superstores to the edges of the city, Danish rules that protect the agrarian lifestyle by insisting that rural homes are actually lived in, and Scottish rules that impose a minimum price per unit of alcohol to decrease alcohol consumption.[2] And so while the principles of mutual recognition and mutual trust were meant as a way to allow Member States to cooperate while respecting the differences between them, it often seems to achieve the exact *opposite*. They have a strongly homogenising effect—wherein differences between Member States disappear due to the obligation of recognising each other's rules.

It is, in fact, in exactly the policy areas where the EU operates on the basis of mutual trust that the EU is most heavily contested. The internal market is seen as a neo-liberal monster that paves over local customs; Member States refuse to extradite criminals to other countries because they do not trust the standards of justice in those countries; and Member States erect border walls to prevent refugees from entering from other countries.[3] The EU's attempt to decrease differences between Europeans is creating *more* rather than less resistance to cooperation.

The reason why the principles of mutual recognition and mutual trust at times seem to lead to their exact opposite is, in the simplest of terms, because they force Member States to do something that they do not necessarily want to do. Finland is forced to accept cucumbers that do not conform to its rules; Slovenia has to allow a Belgian engineer to build bridges even though the engineer was not trained in accordance with Slovenian standards; and the Irish authorities have to arrest and extradite a criminal to Poland despite doubts about the independence of the Polish judiciary. These principles, then, operate to displace local differences in how things are done.

But why is this so problematic? Why does this seem to lead to *distrust*? Just imagine going to the restaurant with a friend. While you are in the bathroom, she orders for you. Even if she chose your favourite dish, you will probably still be a bit nonplussed by her action. If your friend orders something you do *not* like, you'll probably be annoyed at her for having ordered. And if your friend orders something that you are culturally uncomfortable or unfamiliar with, you might start to rethink your friendship. This is hardly rocket science: we understand this without problem on a daily basis. It is, in fact, the reason why you don't order food for your friends when they are in the bathroom.

And yet, the EU has somehow not understood what the Luxembourg school kids did: that pursuing uniformity across Europe is the source of distrust rather than trust. The EU still thinks that diversity somehow inhibits cooperation, and that this diversity must be turned—by hook or crook—into unity, as a way to stabilise the integration project.

As we will see in the next sections, however, the EU has it exactly the wrong way around. Diversity between local 'ways of doing things' is a source of *trust* rather than distrust in Europe. Trust, in fact, operates on the basis of respect for and tolerance of difference—not on the basis of its bulldozing. Diversity is not the headwind that makes European integration more difficult, it is, as the Luxembourg school kids realised, the *very reason why the crew is still on board*! For this to become clear, we should first take a detour to discuss why trust is so central in stabilising political projects.

Why Trust Matters

It is Tuesday, 6 pm. I am cycling home after work, and, on the way back, pick up some groceries from the local supermarket and my son from day care. After the bath and a night-time story, it's time for a meal and a movie on Netflix. An average Tuesday, right? Now think of the amounts of trust that are required to make this—indeed—a straightforward Tuesday: you trust your employer to eventually pay you for work, car drivers not to target your bike, the nursery to take the best care of your son, the supermarket to accept your money and to safeguard food safety standards, fellow shoppers not to push you over, the shampoo to be safe for use, and Netflix not to scan your computer for your credit card details.

We do not think about these actions as being based—fundamentally—on a large degree of personal and institutional trust. All aspects of our lives are imbued with trust, which simplifies almost every action in our lives. It is, without exaggeration, the glue that holds society together. Without trust, in fact, we would struggle to stay sane in the highly complex societies we live in. Unsurprisingly, then, the general absence of trust is linked to numerous physiological disorders, from paranoia to bipolar personality disorder.

But why is trust so important in structuring a society? And why is it so important for a project like the EU? We can think about trust in two ways. Later on in this chapter we will look at how we *learn* to trust. But before we get there, let's see what trust *does*, that is, how it helps to stabilise interactions in a complex society: how it makes the above example a routine Tuesday, rather than a rollercoaster of anxiety.

Trust does two things. On the one hand, it stabilises cooperation between people that do not know each other, and, on the other hand, it makes it easier to deal with differences and disagreement in society.

First, trust allows for cooperation between individuals by stabilising joint commitments and mutual expectations. This sounds complicated, but it is relatively straightforward. Think of cooperation as the rating systems on Uber or Airbnb, which allow us to verify the extent to which we can trust someone that we do not know for the purposes of a specific transaction or interaction. This artificial placeholder for trust (say, a rating of the stranger's trustworthiness between 1 and 5 stars) allows us to cooperate in quite intimate terms—getting into someone's car or renting out one's house—with someone we have never met in our lives. In our daily lives, we operate an even more nuanced and subconscious rating system on a non-stop basis.

Michael Tomasello, a developmental psychologist, has worked with primates and young children to understand why we cooperate, and what role trust plays in individual and group behaviour. His work shows that children around their first birthday cooperate indiscriminately: they are happy to help anyone and share their food with all others. Soon after their first birthday, however, they already start varying the degree to which they trust others dependent on peer feedback, past reciprocity, and the likelihood of future reciprocity. What emerges here is something called 'shared intentionality'. This is an implicit agreement between individuals to achieve a certain purpose—be it to ensure sufficiency of food (in our forefathers), being able to cross the city on a bike without being hit by a car, or the mutually advantageous exchange of services such as with Uber or Airbnb.

Shared intentionality is everywhere around us. Every aspect of our lives, from sexual relationships to mass religion, from book clubs to terrorist organisations to online communities, is based on shared intentionality. What Tomasello has discovered is that this shared intentionality is strongly enforced by individuals from a very young age: actions that contribute to the achievement of a certain shared purpose receive positive feedback, while actions that inhibit this achievement are sanctioned or punished. These feedback structures are very sophisticated. Often a raised eyebrow or a certain look is sufficient to express acceptance or punishment. Humans, who have had to cooperate for millennia, have evolved to subconsciously process even the subtlest of feedbacks. It is this shared intentionality, enforced by all participants, that allows us to cooperate with people that we do not know: it allows me to presume that car drivers are not out to kill me when I cycle past them, and that a supermarket where I've never been will accept my money and not sell poisonous beer. The first reason why trust matters, then, is that it allows us to 'do' things in cooperation with people we do not know, without which modern society would be impossible.

The second reason why trust matters is not because it makes it easier to get things 'done' but because it makes it easier to handle diversity and disagreement in society. Trust, in fact, is indispensible in holding together societies as they become ever more diverse and interdependent. More than ever before, we are dependent on a larger number of people for our basic needs: our food comes from across the globe, our safety depends on sophisticated surveillance operations, the water supply depends on hundreds of people doing their jobs, and the medicine industry employs millions of people across the globe just so that the right medicine is ready for you when you get an ulcer. Just ask your (grand)parents about where food came from when they were young: you will be astonished at how quickly the supply chain has extended beyond relatively stable and local social networks. And, more than ever before, the people that we depend on are more and more diverse: they are no longer from the next village over, but can be based anywhere in the world. We do not share a vision of what life should look like, a cuisine, a value system, a culture, or a language. I have very little in common with the person who designed my smartphone in California, made it in China, or even the local farmer who cultivated the potatoes that I use. Modern society is riddled with interactions between people that do not agree with each other on a thousand different topics. Yet, modern society is—for a large part—highly efficient in making these people cooperate with each other despite all these differences. The reason? Trust.

Trust solves the problem of cooperation with 'others' by, essentially, allowing us to disagree. What trust does, to put it as simply as possible, is to block out the question of agreement on values or interests. We do not need to agree about globalisation, music tastes, or euthanasia with our new neighbour before we decide to buy a flat. We can trust that these differences are unimportant in our capacity to live next to each other in a way that pleases us both. In this sense, trust creates a degree of tolerance and respect for difference and disagreement. Or, to turn this around, disagreement and difference are *not* the enemy of trust. If they were, all cooperation would immediately stop, and only be possible between people who agree with each other on everything. Trust, then, is crucial in allowing us to negotiate differences—in values, power, and interests—by creating a measure of solidarity and civility between individuals, and tolerance and respect for each other's values and traditions.

Work by psychologists suggests, in fact, that as our societies become more complex, and with it the demands of trust more elaborate, we are becoming more tolerant and more respectful of difference. Empirical work by Charles Heckscher, for example, shows that the commitment to values of tolerance and respect have risen sharply since the 1980s, and particularly so in millennials, whose interactions with 'others' are infinitely greater than those of the previous generations.[4] The second reason why trust matters, then, is because it allows us to skirt disagreement: it creates cohesion in a society where there is no other basis for it.

It is not surprising that all political projects, be it the nation state or the EU, are interested in trust. Trust allows for cooperation between strangers; it creates loyalty and commitment to pursue common objectives; and it creates cohesion in a complex and highly diverse society. In the European context, the importance of trust cannot be overstated. To put it crudely, trust between European citizens reduces the complexity of cooperation between the 27 Member States with radically different traditions, ideas, and values infinitely more than any regulatory programme dreamt up by the European Commission.

But trust can never be blind or presumed. If my neighbour turns out to be a ruthless gangster, I will no longer give him my spare key. If a friend keeps ordering food for me in the restaurant, I may no longer accept her invitations to go out. Or, to put a European spin to it, if Spanish cucumbers are poisonous, Finnish consumers might no longer buy them. Trust might be useful to bridge differences between Europeans, and to allow people to cooperate despite those differences, but it still requires a *source*. And these sources of trust, invariably, have to do with people interacting with each other. This is where the EU is making its main mistake. As we saw in the previous section, much of the EU's logic is based on the fundamental premise that the source for trust in European integration is increasing the *similarity* between the different parts of Europe. As we will see in the next section, however, the main sources of trust are *not* based on similarity, but based on (interaction between) difference.

How We Learn to Trust

Trusting someone is not a rational or deliberate exercise. We might sometimes consciously decide whether or not to trust a taxi driver's rate, or whether someone offering to sell a bike has in fact stolen it. But this is not the type of trust that we are concerned with here, when we think of large-scale cooperation between a diverse range of individuals. Learning to trust, in this setting, is a highly nuanced and sophisticated process. It has evolved over the course of hundreds and thousands of years, in such a way as to fit the human environment. Trust is expressed and consolidated by a number of social conventions and practices that we no longer associate with it: think of handshakes, eye contact, intonation, or the practice of gossiping. Nevertheless it is important to distinguish at least three general ways in which we *learn* to trust. These are specific to trusting people beyond one's primary group of socialisation—that is, beyond the people in your immediate vicinity. As such, they shed light on how trust emerges in the complex setting such as the EU, and what we may be able to do to stimulate its development.

The first source of trust is interdependence. Michael Tomasello, in his work with young children and chimpanzees, argues that 'awareness of interdependence leads to social normativity of rational action'.[5] What this means is that once individuals appreciate how interdependent they are, their actions change. Our forefathers, when they were hunting, depended on each other for directions, to distract the animals, warn each other of dangers, and had to cooperate to kill bigger animals. In these conditions, trust is indispensable. When your own survival, your access to food, shelter, income, or the well-being of your children is dependent on the actions of others, something changes in your interaction with them. What happens is that individuals start to be sensitive to each other's needs, that they craft roles and reciprocal expectations and obligations, and that they solidify their interactions in social conventions and institutions. We do not think of trust when you shake someone's hand, automatically track the eye sightline of people in close proximity, when we think of parliaments, prisons, or email—but these are all advanced examples of the systematisation of trust. Charles Tilly, in his work on trust networks and their integration in democratic structures (we will come back to him), argues in fact that this is precisely the reason why the first sophisticated trust networks dealt with the management of our immediate live world: from water control to procreation, from food sourcing to cohabitation. It is *because* we have always been interdependent in these areas that we have learned to trust in these settings.

And as interdependence in modern society increases and relationships become more complex, so does trust. Today, when most of us (myself included) have no idea how it is that potable water runs out of the tap when we open it, or how supermarkets manage to stock a mind-blowing diversity of food sourced from around the globe, trust is perpetually implied. In living in our highly complex world, we continuously engage in the reproduction and stabilisation of these ties of interdependence and trust. We trust that water will run out of the tap tomorrow and will not kill us, that trains will run next week, and supermarkets continue to be stocked. In continually making these assumptions, we also continually stabilise this first source of trust. Trust is, to use more difficult terms, generative and performative: when we trust *in action*, we learn to trust *even more*. These forms of trust—based on thick forms of interdependence—exist also beyond face-to-face interaction. Think of the neighbourhood councils that spontaneously have emerged in Barcelona in the past years and perform tasks, such as childcare, food production, or cleaning, that the public authorities cannot adequately provide anymore. Or think of cooperation between states to launch satellites into space, simulate the big bang in particle accelerators, or, indeed, think of the European Union. The interdependence between the EU's Member States is such that, say, Slovenia or Denmark cannot meaningfully fight climate change without the support of their neighbours. *Awareness* of this type of interdependence, in other words, is crucial in creating trust between Danish, Slovenian, Maltese, and Polish citizens. This first source of trust, then, suggests that European integration would be stabilised much more by solving collective problems than by creating homogeneity between them.

The second source of trust is not premised on interdependence between individuals as much as it is about interaction between them. It is not based on a need to cooperate or work together, but on understanding and getting to know a person that is different from you. An example of this that is often used in literature or cinema is that of the racist worker having to come to terms with his new black boss, or a strongly religious grandmother having to deal with the gay friends of her granddaughter that come to stay for a weekend. What these storylines play with is the process that people go through when they are faced with the unknown, or, in academic language, the 'other'. The grandmother is forced to deal with her prejudices against gay people when she actually encounters them. Whether the interaction ends up reinforcing, nuancing, or overthrowing her own beliefs doesn't matter: the interaction with the 'other' inevitably shapes her.

The 'other' is an important psychological concept. It is used primarily to describe how we become who we are. In very simple terms, we become who we are by interacting with things that we are *not*, in the sense that we create a space of personal freedom by acting autonomously from certain imposed visions of identity. This may sound counterintuitive, but just think about how central issues such as nationality, religion, food preferences, loyalty to sports teams, or social classes are to the construction of one's identity. All these identities are framed as much by what one is *not* than by what one is. Being Belgian means not being Spanish; being vegetarian means not eating meat; being a Muslim means not being Jewish; just like being a Spurs fan means not being an Arsenal fan, and so on.

In our contemporary world, more than ever, we are exposed to people who are different from us—the 'others'. And this interaction is interesting from the perspective of trust. Because the more we get to know about the 'other', the more we appreciate their choices—not in the sense that we become *like* them or agree with them (we may even become *less* like them) but in the sense that we appreciate that the 'other' is who she is because of the same range of personal choices that we ourselves have made. And these types of interactions matter because they make the difference between people tangible and visible, and, importantly, less scary: familiarity breeds trust.

Many scholars have worked on this question of difference in society. Jane Addams, for example, around 1900 already showed that problems of difference in the construction of trust and cooperation can to a large extent be solved by doing everyday, mundane, activities together: parenting, shopping, sharing food. These types of activities show basic patterns of similarity, even if how you parent or what you buy in the shop is radically different from your neighbour. Mundane interaction with 'the others' demystifies them and makes it easier to understand their motives and choices. In the Europe of today, this translates into even more mundane things: a Polish boy watching the Champions League match between Liverpool and Roma; an Irish teacher who has two Estonian kids in his class; a Portuguese woman eating Belgian fries or watching an online clip of a gaffe on German TV that has gone viral. These might sound like silly examples, but are real, everyday ways in which the 'other' becomes tangible. As Charles Herschel, one of the first scholars to work on trust in the age of the internet, highlights, this kind of interaction is not purely commercial, functional, or trite, but carries in it 'exchanges about culture, values and aesthetics—the aspects of human life that enable people to understand each other better'.[6]

The perfect example of this in the European context is the Eurovision song contest. I doubt this has ever made anymore feel more European, or made anyone feel more closely connected to a neighbouring state. In fact, it probably makes one feel *more* of a national. But that is exactly the point: it is a celebration of *difference* that nevertheless allows us to understand the other better. The work of sociologist Richard Sennett on rituals is very instructive in this regard. He argues that rituals serve to make cooperation (and trust, in fact) easier because they diminish fear, envy, and jealousy. Instead, he argues, 'ritualized moments which celebrate the differences between members of a community, which affirm the distinctive value of each person, can diminish the acid of invidious comparison and promote cooperation'.[7] Simply *understanding* that individuals or countries *are* different, then, generates trust because we learn more about each other and each other's motivations and choices. It is through the most mundane of interactions in Europe, then, both in real life and online, through the food we eat and the TV programmes we watch, that trust emerges between Europeans. It is, then, not in overcoming but in *celebrating* the differences between Europeans that we can locate a source of trust.

The third source of trust is based around sharing common projects. An example of this is asking a random passer-by to help push your car onto the pavement. There is little interdependence in this interaction—if the passer-by is in a rush, you can ask one of the next ten people that pass. What takes place, however, in such an occurrence, is the creation of shared intentionality. We saw this term before in this chapter, when we discussed why trust is so important for political projects. Shared intentionality, we saw, allows strangers to cooperate by focusing on a *specific* goal that is to be achieved. If you and the random passer-by want to push the car onto the pavement, this presumes that you will not merely pretend to push, and that you will not have secretly jammed the wheels. This example is similar to what happens when large groups of individuals (or states) undertake a common project. Think of the behaviour of the thousands of people in close proximity in a public transport, at festivals, or sport events: the way in which they interact, queue, pass, make space for each other is all tied to the *purpose* of the interaction. Historically, concepts such as religion and the nation state have used 'shared intentionality' as a way to produce trust and consolidate relationships between independent individuals. A devout Christian in Bari is in no way dependent on a priest in Galway; but the trust between them emerges from the fact that they engage in a common project. In the Europe of today, the capacity of concepts like religion or nationality to mobilise large groups of people is rapidly diminishing—partially due to an increased heterogeneity of residents and religious affiliations, and partially due to an explosion of other loyalties that may conflict with the demands of religion and nationality: class, sexuality, gender, political affiliation, leisure, food, and so on.

The EU has also long operated on the basis of 'shared intentionality'. The way in which its institutions are structured, the way in which the roles between them have been divided, and the scope of its power has always revolved around its central purpose: the achievement of 'peace and prosperity'. After the Second World War, this was a purpose, a shared project, around which all Member States could rally, and, therefore, a source of trust between Europeans. The same applies to the admissions of new Member States in southern and eastern Europe, all of which joined the EU after a period of authoritarian rule. The creation of the shared intentionality of 'peace and prosperity' does not mean that all participants agree on how to achieve this purpose (there are more than one method to get the car onto the pavement, after all), but it serves to focus attention and disagreement around the common project. Trust is generated, in these instances, because of the implied acceptance of the purpose as being relevant and meaningful.

Political communities, including the EU, increasingly struggle to create such common visions of the future that can inspire trust between its participants. The increased apathy and disengagement from politics is partially due to this lack of centrifugal force that shared intentionality can engender. The surprising thing in this story, however, is that it is not very difficult to imagine political projects that could be the source of trust among its participants. The battle against climate change and the impact of technological advances on the way our societies operate are projects that could create this focus and will be discussed in more depth in the next chapter.

But we could also think of shared European projects that we *already* take for granted. Angela Merkel famously keeps repeating that while Europe has 7% of the global population, and it has 25% of its GDP, it represents 50% of global spending on welfare. For Merkel, this is a problem: how can we compete with countries across the world that mistreat their citizens and can thereby produce cheaper goods? We could also think of these numbers as an incredible achievement of what is clearly a common project that most Member States share: the need to protect the most vulnerable in society, and to offer their citizens a life that is not contingent on their capacity to be a successful actor in a capitalist market society. Focusing the citizens' attention on these very general common projects has the potential to create trust networks across borders because it indicates a *reason* for cooperation and simultaneously facilitates its achievement by clarifying the direction of travel and the policy implications. If I agree to help get the car onto the pavement, after all, I both contribute to achieving this objective and understand my responsibilities in the process. This third source of trust, then, once again does *not* presume similarity or uniformity between Europeans. It does, however, require common projects that transcend those differences.

In the complex society in which we live, trust is invaluable. It makes cooperation between strangers possible and creates the tolerance for difference and solidarity without which life would be even more stressful. In this section, we saw that trust can emerge in different ways, and that difference between individuals is in no way inimical to their capacity to cooperate or trust each other. This is an important lesson for the EU. Interactions between Europeans and shared projects are much more important for our desire to cooperate than the question whether or not we all 'feel' European. The idea that similarity between Europeans, or that some sort of European identity is necessary before we can trust each other and move forward with the integration project is a blind alley, and a dangerous one at that.

Trust and the EU

The three sources of trust that were identified in the previous section suggest that there is more to the narrative of trust in Europe than we usually assume. The caricature of distrusting, scheming neighbours is one that is increasingly inaccurate. As we become more aware of how much we depend on each other, and as we get to know each other better, the reservoirs of trust are filling up. This does not mean that more and more Europeans trust the EU, or trust each other's governments. Empirical research routinely shows that Europeans trust citizens from other states much more than they trust any government (including their own). This is not surprising if we take account of the sources of trust discussed in the previous section.

But while much research has looked into trust *within* nations, there is less research about trust between citizens *across* nations. There are reasons for optimism, however. The proportion of Europeans working abroad—whether temporary or permanently—has never been higher. The proportion of Europeans travelling to other Member States has never been higher. The chances of you interacting with a fellow European on the work floor, in the lecture hall, in the neighbourhood, in the shop, or at the school gates are, likewise, higher than ever. This is so in the cosmopolitan hubs such as Amsterdam, Barcelona, or Berlin, but increasingly also in Cluj, Lyon, or Gdansk. The free movement of goods has brought products from all over Europe to our supermarkets: pizza—just a few generations ago considered an exotic Italian speciality—is now ubiquitous, as are Belgian beer or French cheese. The football stars of Real Madrid are Belgian, Croatian, and German as well as Spanish. These mundane interactions with 'Europe'—whether in the form of your children's play dates, cooperating at work, eating Italian food, or adoring a Croatian football player, matter: they are not simple commercial or mundane transactions, but imply and stabilise the expression of trust.

If we look at it from this perspective, trust between Europeans is in plentiful supply, and interactions between Europeans will only increase due to technological advances and the increased ease in mobility. This does not mean that such interaction is decreasing the diversity of Europe, that it is somehow homogenising European culture. Interactions such as the ones sketched above, serve, as we saw, as a way to convey *difference*: to make people sensitive to what is unique about themselves and what makes 'others' themselves. These interactions create trust by making difference subordinate to what we share: while we may speak different languages and greet our children in different ways at the school gates, our children still share a classroom. Even though Luka Modrić doesn't look Spanish and speaks mangled Spanish, he still works hard for the local team that many Madrilenians support: Real Madrid. Cooperation and interaction do not bulldoze difference; they make it manageable.

But not all is well with trust in Europe. While Europeans might become more sensitive to each other's quirks and needs, this is only the starting point for the consolidation of trust. For trust to lead to stable cooperation, and to the creation of 'shared intentionality', trust needs to be institutionalised. This does not only entail creating political institutions such as parliaments or governments, but also social institutions and conventions that become a container of these new sources of trust. When the modern nation states were consolidated, for example, shared history, language, and culture served this function: it created a narrative, or a purpose, that somehow linked the Sicilian factory worker with the Piemontese goat farmer. The EU, clearly, struggles to institutionalise the trust that exists between its citizens. In fact, where it does attempt to institutionalise trust, for example, through homogenising market interactions or by creation of a European Constitution, it is as likely to breed mistrust as trust.

This paradox offers three insights. First, it tells us that the EU, and specifically the rules that govern the marketplace, must become more sensitive to the diversity that Europe offers. This diversity comes in many forms and guises—from the way we act to what we consume, and from the way we communicate to our cultural habits—and is closely tied to the way in which the local environment has evolved through historical, geographical, or cultural circumstances. The starting point in making Europeans trust each other more, then, is simply to respect the existing diversity, and even highlight it.

The second lesson from this chapter is that the EU requires more common projects that can engender passion and engagement, and that can offer a shared ambition for all Europeans. The EU's project of 'peace and prosperity' played this role in the first decades after the war: this goal was so widely shared among a decimated population living in a ravaged continent that 'shared intentionality' was not difficult to establish. It is a measure of the success of the integration project that this ambition of 'peace and prosperity' no longer enthuses its citizens. The challenge of developing new ambitions for the European Union, particularly geared for the younger generations of Europeans, which is taken up in the next chapter, is absolutely indispensable in the institutionalisation of trust between Europeans. To put it simply, we must have *reasons* to cooperate and trust each other.

The third insight that follows from this chapter is that the problem of the EU is not that Europeans do not trust each other, but the EU's incapacity of *politically* institutionalising that trust. As Charles Tilly has shown in his research, trust networks can stabilise a political project only when they are integrated in the way a government works. This may sound complicated, and we will devote a whole chapter on working through its implications. What it means, in the simplest terms, is that a government, if it is to be successful, must learn to use the trust between its citizens, and commit the citizens to the fate of the polity. Institutionalising trust, in this sense, is a very delicate process. Most scholars, in fact, suggest that the main limit to cooperation between citizens is not trust between them (which is in more plentiful supply than we might expect), but, rather, the way we can translate this trust into government. Richard Sennett, for example, ends his book-length study on cooperation with the statement that 'as social animals we are capable of trusting and cooperating much more deeply than the existing social order envisions'.[8] It falls on us, then, to think how we might reform the EU's institutions in a way that allows for a more sophisticated engagement with the manifold ways that the integration process has changed the interactions between its citizens.

CONCLUSION

We started this chapter with a quote by a former Austrian chancellor, who compared the diversity of Europe with a headwind—making it harder to advance the sailing boat of European integration. The EU, in this narrative, must try to overcome the divide in customs, habits, and rules that prevents meaningful cooperation. It is difficult to overstate how dangerous and counterproductive this view of European integration is, even though it is widely shared among its leaders. Europe has a glorious diversity of local customs, languages, cuisines, and, generally, 'ways of living'. The way in which parents and children talk to each other differs radically between Naples and Helsinki. What happens when colleagues go for lunch is very different in Rotterdam and in Bordeaux. 'Going for a drink' or 'having breakfast' means different things in Thessaloniki, Cork, and Prague. The point of this chapter has been to show that the great variety of customs and traditions in the EU is its great strength, not its weakness. Trust and cooperation are premised on respect for difference, not its eradication. But challenging existing customs and traditions *in the name of cooperation* will only breed—and has bred—distrust between Europeans and resistance to cooperation rather than the opposite.

NOTES

1. Le Soir, 'Une devise de compromis pour l'Europe (5 May 2000), retrieved at https://www.cvce.eu/obj/a_compromise_motto_for_europe_from_le_soir_5_may_2000-en-1c07fdf3-a867-4b64-bafe-22b653b1ad82.html
2. Case C-148/15, *Deutsche Parkinson* ECLI:EU:C:2016:776; Case C-360/15, *Appingedam* ECLI:EU:C:2018:44; Case C-400/08, *European Commission v Spain* ECLI:EU:C:2011:172; Case C-370/05, *Festersen* ECLI:EU:C:2007: 59; and Case C-333/14, *Scotch Whisky* ECLI:EU:C: 2015:845.
3. Joined Cases C-411/10 and C-493/10, *N.S.* ECLI:EU:C:2011:865; and Case C-216/18 (PPU), *LM* ECLI:EU:C: 2018:586.

4. C. Herschel, *Trust in a Complex World* (Oxford University Press, 2015), 94–95.
5. M. Tomasello, *Why We Cooperate* (Boston Review, 2009), 90.
6. C. Herschel, *Trust in a Complex World* (Oxford University Press, 2015), 74.
7. R. Sennett, *Together: The Rituals, Pleasures and Politics of Cooperation* (Penguin, 2013), 82.
8. R. Sennett, *Together: The Rituals, Pleasures and Politics of Cooperation* (Penguin, 2013), 280.

CHAPTER 4

Aspirations

Every year, a company called GFK Global publishes an extensive study entitled 'Nation Brand Index'. This ranks the reputation of countries across the globe, on matters such as competence of the institutions, the quality and reputation of the products produced in that country, available culture and heritage, innovation and the perceived qualities of the people in those countries—ranging from helpfulness and creativity to tolerance. Using the answers from thousands of people across the globe, this index lists how different countries are perceived across the globe, that is, how 'strong' their brand is. The strength of a brand matters, simply put, because it facilitates all aspects of cooperation: a strong 'nation brand' will attract more tourists, highly skilled workers, direct investment, and obtain more favourable trade conditions; while its products, workers, and cultural trends tend to be popular abroad. In 2018, for example, Germany and Japan were the strongest nation 'brands', while the United States and the United Kingdom have declined significantly in the past years as a result of the election of Trump and Brexit.

In 2006, the Nation Brand Index—led by Simon Anholt, a British policy advisor who has worked for decades on the perceptions of nations—included a guest: the European Union. Surprisingly, given the Euroscepticism that was already spreading across the EU's own Member States, the EU came first in the ranking—comfortably outranking every other nation tested. To some extent, this makes sense. As Simon Anholt himself put it: 'few places in the world could be more attractive than a

© The Author(s) 2020
F. de Witte, *re:generation Europe*,
https://doi.org/10.1007/978-3-030-19788-9_4

composite of Italy plus France plus the UK plus Germany plus Sweden, and so forth'.[1] If we look more closely at the data, in fact, it becomes clear that people across the globe rate the EU for its exports, its culture, tourism, and its investment and innovation strategies. At the same time, the EU ranked much lower in the categories that measure the quality and effectiveness of its governance. What this shows, Anholt argues, is the gulf of difference between *Europe as a continent* and *Europe as an institution*. Even though the study asked for people's perceptions on the European Union, most interviewees took this to mean Europe as a geographical place—with its diversity in cultures, products, and tourism possibilities. Only when asked questions about governance, did the interviewees switch their focus to the European *Union*. This outcome shouldn't surprise the reader that has made it to this point in this book: the European Union—this particular institutional echo of Europe—is not particularly good at capturing what Europe actually *is*.

After having read this report, I became intrigued with what brand theory (which is mostly preoccupied with building, solidifying, or saving the reputation of commercial brands) might be able to teach us about this fundamental mismatch. Why is it that Europe is a much easier 'sell' than the EU? And how might the EU become *more like Europe*—the continent that it is meant to represent? Most of the basic principles of branding theory do not apply to cities, nations, or regional organisations for the simple reason that no one can ever have full control over the content, quality, and consistency of these 'nation products'—in a way that, say, Carlsberg or Siemens can have full control over the taste of their beer or the functioning of their dishwasher. Instead, what matters most for the branding of places is *acting in the way you want to be seen*. This might seem a misleadingly simple statement, but all research shows that it is impossible to create a strong reputation—whether in products produced, the friendliness of inhabitants, quality of tourism destinations, or the effectiveness of government when, in fact, your products are flawed, inhabitants rude, and the government corrupt. This is the case for the EU's reputation across the globe, but, of course, doubly so for its reputation with its *own* citizens, who will have much more awareness of the EU's strengths and weaknesses.

The disaffection with the EU across the continent has grown significantly over the past decades. In part, this is fuelled by its response to the Euro-crisis and the refugee crisis, but also, as Brexit demonstrated, its rules on free movement, its impact on the welfare state, and its democratic pedigree. These Eurosceptic narratives are now almost a staple in general elections across the EU, with hard-left and hard-right parties reaping the benefits from this disaffection. But what does the growing discontent actually tell us about the EU? Or, to put a branding spin on the question: what would a branding agency do if the EU were to ask it to strengthen its reputation? How could the EU 'sell' itself to the citizen, and make sure that the citizens remain committed to the integration project?

The first thing that a branding agency would tell the EU when faced with such an unenviable request is that the EU needs a coherent narrative. This means that the EU needs to offer a specific vision of the future and a clear common purpose that its citizens can identify with and rally around. This common purpose should, in turn, inform how the EU organises itself internally, how it acts, and—thereby—how it is perceived by its citizenry. At the focal point of this magic formula is the idea of a common purpose, of a certain *aspiration* about how the future should look.

This chapter discusses what these aspirations might be, and why they are so crucial for the EU's future. It does so from a generational perspective, focusing on the younger generations—the millennials, and Generation Z, and the Generation α (Alpha). These generations offer an interesting paradox for the EU. On the one hand, they are 'EU-natives'. They have known the EU their whole lives, they will have crossed borders and used the Euro most of their lives, and will have travelled and cooperated with fellow Europeans more extensively than any generation before them. They are, in other words, already more European than most of their ancestors, and—as empirical work shows—generally more positively predisposed towards the integration project. On the other hand, it does not seem that the EU is doing much on the issues that matter for these generations: youth unemployment has never been higher, we are told that the generous welfare state that our parents became used to is untenable for our generations, owning a house—the most basic assertion of independence by our parents—is becoming a pipedream for most of us, and we have inherited a climate that is about to lead to a global meltdown. The message from this chapter is, therefore, very simple. If the EU wants to remain relevant for its younger generations (and the other way around!), then the EU will need to become more sensitive to the aspirations of those generations. Only by articulating a common purpose that enthuses these generations does the EU stand a chance of making the brand 'EU' as strong and attractive as the brand 'Europe'.

WHY ASPIRATIONS MATTER

Why are a polity's aspirations so crucial in 'selling' itself to the citizen? It seems odd to discuss what the common purpose of, say, Slovenia or Austria is. Usually, we do not think of polities such as nation states as serving a particular purpose. Why, then, is it so crucial that we answer the question what the point is of the European Union? The reason is that there are two distinct ways in which polities can 'sell' themselves. With 'selling', I mean that polities seek to inspire loyalty, commitment, and engagement from the citizens.

The first way of selling a polity is by creating what is called a 'community of fate'. These are social fabrications that tell a story that links the citizens to a particular geographical location and to each other. We are all familiar with these narratives, which often rely on shared culture, history, ethnicity, language, or a shared struggle, plight, or acts of heroism. Almost all modern-day European nation states are built on this foundation. If we look at the map of Europe in 1600, for example, just 400 years ago, we immediately see that not a single EU Member State existed in its current form. When the modern nation states were created, then, they sought to 'sell' themselves to their citizens by relying on an explicit mix of buying loyalty from the influential landowners, forcing a single language on the subjects, rewriting historical narratives, and integrating different parts of the nation into a single economic system. We now take for granted that Italy, France, and Germany are separate nations with their particular 'way of living' and with their independent cultural and historical narratives, but we often forget that these are all social fabrications. They are constructed identities. This is not to say that social fabrications do not matter, quite the opposite: they matter a lot. It is these social fabrications that connect a shepherd in Alto Adige with a factory worker in Palermo, and make them feel part of the same community, and make them willing to cooperate and share resources, even though they have never met and might never meet.

A second way of 'selling' a polity is not by constructing a shared history and identity, but by offering a certain image of a collective or shared future. A good example of this approach is the United States, or the Soviet Union: these political projects were as much experiments in new ways of living together as anything else. In these projects, then, what draws people together—from Wisconsin to Arizona, or from Leningrad to Osh—is not a shared past, but a shared aspiration: a desire to construct a world in which certain values and objectives are absolutely central. These aspirations, in turn, serve not only to 'sell' the polity to its citizens but also to tell us something about how the polity should be constructed: what the rights and obligations of the citizens and the state should be. In the long run the common objective even becomes part of the fabric of the polity and the self-understanding and identity of the citizens. The vision of the 'American dream', for example, is one that can be traced back to the common purpose of the construction of the United States—in defiance of the more regimented and class-based European societies—but one that has become, over the centuries, part of how the United States actually operates and the way citizens see themselves and their country.

In our daily lives, we are comfortable with both ways in which identity, loyalty, and commitment are constructed. I am Belgian, and even though I have never lived there, I do feel connected to the polity because of stories of my parents' youth, my language, holidays as a child, TV-shows, and contact with extended family members. Religion works in similar ways: it offers a historical narrative that breeds loyalty from people across the globe—from Havana to Kinshasa—that would otherwise have little in common. These are examples of the first way of creating commitment between citizens: they are based on historical narratives that link people together based on a shared (and often constructed) past. Examples of the second way of creating commitment between citizens are also all around us in our daily lives: think of any club that you may want to join. Whether it's a book club, a volleyball team, a non-governmental organisation (NGO), or a terrorist organisation, they are all structured around a certain aspiration or common purpose. It is the purpose *itself*—be it to discuss about books, win in sporting contests, or change the world in a specific way—that creates loyalty and commitment from the participants.

Aspirations, in other words, matter because they can substitute for political projects that base themselves on strong or 'thick' historical identities. This is something that is often overlooked in the EU context. Many politicians, academics, and lawyers have argued that the integration project is ultimately doomed to fail because there is no such thing as a European identity. Europe is too diverse for the creation of one kind of identity: too many languages, too many 'ways of doing things', too many different historical narratives, ethic features, and social sensibilities. Because of this diversity, the argument goes, the EU can never 'sell' itself like nation states can. Part of this criticism is true: the EU can never 'sell' itself in *exactly the same way* as the nation state can. But that is also not necessary or even desirable. It would be a crime if the EU would seek—through force or more subtle forms—to decrease the diversity of life on the European continent. As we saw earlier, it is exactly this diversity that is Europe's strongest selling point. Instead, the EU must 'sell' itself to its citizen on the basis of a vision of our collective and shared future. It needs, to put it as simply as possible, a common purpose that can enthuse its citizens and can generate loyalty and commitment to the achievement of this common purpose.

As we will see in the following section, the EU used to have such a common purpose. In the decades after the economic, moral, and infrastructural devastation of the Second World War, the EU's aspiration of creating 'peace and prosperity' served to generate loyalty from the citizens. It was, in other words, a project that 'sold' the EU to its citizens. Today, however, it seems that this aspiration is no longer sufficiently appealing—in part because of the EU's very success. What is needed, then, is a new project that tackles the issues that the new generations face and offer a more appealing vision of our collective future than one without the EU in it.

The EU's Aspirations

It is hard to overstate the mess that Europe was in in 1945. Cities across the continent had been razed to the ground—from Warsaw to Rotterdam and Dresden—and an estimated 18 million residents of the current EU Member States had died, bringing loss and devastation home to almost all families in Europe. The economies of the European nations had collapsed due to the war effort, and there was a general shortage of food, housing, and medicine. Beyond these immediate risks of hunger, homelessness, and sickness lurked the moral bankruptcy of the concentration camps and collaboration. Europe was, for lack of better words, on its knees. It took over $12 billion (in today's money this equates to €90 billion) in aid through the Marshall Plan and years of reconstruction to get the continent back on its feet in economic terms.

But the economic recovery was always going to be the easiest. What about the political and moral reconstruction? This is where the project of European integration comes in. From the outset, however, it is crucial to highlight that the revolutionary project of European cooperation was founded on the need to prevent a repetition of the Second World War more than it was an attempt to construct a European state. As the historian Tony Judt puts it in his seminal study on Europe's post-war period, 'post-national, welfare-state, cooperative, pacific Europe was not born of the optimistic, ambitious, forward-looking project imagined in fond ret-rospect by today's Euro-idealists. It was the insecure child of anxiety.'[2]

The aspirational narrative that followed from this sense of anxiety was one that brought together two objectives, which together gave purpose to the cooperation between the Member States: the pursuit of peace and prosperity. This aspiration made it easy to 'sell' the integration project to the citizens of the—then six—Member States. And the citizens did not buy a cat in a sack: the integration project *did* in fact work hard at making Europe more peaceful and more prosperous. In the last 60 years, there has been no war between the EU's Member States—something unthinkable in the decades and centuries that preceded the integration project. Nor have the Member States ever been more prosperous. A rough estimate of the contribution of the single market to the EU's GDP puts it at 600 bil-lion (or 4% of the GDP). If a survivor of the war in 1945 would have been offered the peaceful and prosperous Europe of today he would not just have bitten your hand off, but eaten you to your bare bones.

The success of the EU's pursuit of its aspirational objective is, today, its problem. It has been wildly successful, and, as a result, its message has lost purchase. The award of the Nobel Peace Prize to the EU in 2012, for example, took most of my students by surprise. For them, war in Europe was just as unthinkable as the EU's involvement in preventing it. Hardly any of the younger generations of Europeans have lived through a war or felt the personal devastation of its effects. In fact, even most of our parents have not. We have grown up with material abundance and—even if very real poverty still exists in Europe—the continent has never been richer in absolute or relative terms. We have entertainment, food, and primary resources in abundance. The risk of war or poverty is not felt widely enough to allow the EU to make its prevention its primary objective. The EU, in a sense, has committed aspirational suicide: the common objective that made it an easy 'sell' to the citizens in the 1950s is no longer relevant today.

This is not a surprise to people working on EU affairs. In fact, the EU has for years attempted to redefine itself in ways that offer a new purpose, or a new aspirational paradigm. One attempt was to go about it by creat-ing some of the instruments that have worked to 'sell' nation states to their citizens: the creation of a European Constitution, with all the hall-marks that one associates with the nation state, such as an official holiday, motto, flag, and so forth. This 'product' failed quite spectacularly when both the French and Dutch voters decided *not* to buy it. Ever since, the EU is trying to sell itself by insisting that it makes the citizens' life easier.

New technical regulations relating to cross-border healthcare, compensation for delayed air travel, a decrease in roaming charges, and the abolishing of daylight savings have been celebrated as the high tide of the new aspirations of the EU. But this does not enthuse the citizenry either, and rightly so: is it possible to invent a more depressing aspiration than slightly cheaper access to WhatsApp when on holiday?

On the occasion of the sixtieth anniversary of the integration project in 2017, the Commission launched five proposals for the future of the EU. The purpose was to find a new aspirational purpose for the EU. In the words of the Commission President Jean-Claude Juncker, 'the European Union has changed our lives for the better. We must ensure that it keeps doing so for all those that follow us.'[3] Even in the most ambitious of those five scenarios, entitled 'doing much more together', the EU's aspirations include 'using connected cars seamlessly across Europe', the creation of a European Monetary Fund, and the replacement of (some) national embassies by European ones in (some) third countries. Is this really the best we can think of? It is not difficult to imagine why more and more voters are returning the EU that they were sold to the shop for a refund: there is very little substance to be found.

Let me wheel out the insights from brand theory once more. The EU should heed two basic lessons very carefully. The first is that you cannot sell what the citizen doesn't want. The second lesson is that you cannot sell a vision or aspiration that you do not deliver on. In 1945, peace and prosperity counted as something that the citizen not just wanted, but needed. And it was an aspiration that the EU delivered on. Today, the aspiration of 'making the citizens' lives easier' is neither wanted nor needed by those citizens, and the 'seamless use of connected cars' falls, how shall we say it, somewhat short of any aspirational vision of our collective future. All this leads us to the question that informs the rest of the chapter: what aspirational vision of our collective future can the EU offer that is needed by its citizenry—and specifically its younger generations—*and* that can be delivered by the EU?

GENERATION EUROPE

This book pays close attention to the relationship between the integration project and the generations born, roughly, between 1981 and 2025: the millennials, Generation Z, and Generation α. Defining generations is clearly a somewhat silly and artificial business. There is no consensus about the exact starting and cutting off points between generations; nor is there any meaningful agreement about the particular traits that a certain generation is supposed to have. Why it is nevertheless useful to speak of generations is the context within which they grow up. Collective and shared experiences that whole generations go through while growing up *do* change the way in which they see the world, their sensitivities, and the way in which they want to live together. A childhood or adolescence spent hiding from bombs, spent in an economic boom, or spent with ubiquitous internet access *does* affect the way in which the citizen sees herself, fellow citizens, and society. Likewise, the traumas of one's parents (and their generation) have an influence on their children's generation. The first scholars to have studied so-called generational theory, William Strauss and Neil Howe, in fact, argue that it operates as a cyclical process, in which children respond to both the context within which they grew up *and* the way in which their parents understand the world.

It is not an overstatement to claim that these three generations will decide the future of the European Union. If the EU cannot 'sell' itself to these groups, it will collapse or, more likely, slowly disintegrate. If we look more closely at the data that is emerging on the perceptions of these generations of the EU, we see something that is both remarkable and troubling for the EU, leaving it with a conundrum that is not easily solved. On the one hand, these generations are easily the most pro-European that we have seen so far. On the other hand, they are unconvinced by the narrative of peace and prosperity—in fact, exactly *because* they were brought up in a period of peace and prosperity in Europe. Instead, they face significant challenges that the EU is not engaging with at all (and, increasingly, see the EU as exacerbating those challenges rather than solving them). These generations will be the most important electoral force in a matter of decades—giving the EU precious little time to make good use of the Euro-positive predisposition of these generations.

Numerous studies have identified that younger generations are more positively predisposed to the integration project than the older ones. Perhaps the most revealing of these studies, commissioned by the Bertelsmann Foundation, has looked at the perception of the EU of people that acknowledged that they know little or nothing about the EU.[4] In older Europeans, support for the EU drops to 44% for this category. In millennials, on the other hand, support for the EU sits at 60% *even for those individuals who know nothing about the EU*. The reason for this is simply that for these generations, the EU is a social fact, that is, a fact of life.

Something that is *presumed* to exist, not something that was born and can die. The same study found a majority of 65% of all young Europeans in favour of more cooperation and more solidarity. The Brexit vote, likewise, showed some astonishing generational divisions. Of the voters under 24, for example, a whopping 75% voted in favour of staying in the EU. What all these figures show, quite simply, is that the younger generations are ready to embrace European integration and the EU. They are, to go back to our branding metaphor, ready to translate their commitment and loyalty into 'buying' the EU's project.

The problem is, however, that they are not willing to buy what the EU is *currently* selling. Almost every European under 35 struggles more than their parents in finding a job, affording a house, and paying for education, childcare, and pensions. There is a genuine possibility that—for the first time since 1945—the members of millennials, Generation Z, and Generation α will be less well-off than their parents. The contrast could not be bigger, in fact. The baby-boom generation grew up in a time of abundant and cheap housing stock, free education, generous welfare payments, and *labour* scarcity. This is unimaginable for the younger generations today. Youth unemployment in Spain has been above 35% since 2009, with a peak of 54% in 2013. This means that *one in two* young adults found no job whatsoever, and the other half tended to work significantly below their qualities and level of education. The research foundation *Bruno Visentini* calculated that the average age at which an Italian can make ends meet without support of their parents in allowances or housing was 30 years in 2004, but is expected to rise to 38 in 2020 and even 48 in 2030.[5] The biggest generation in most European states, the baby-boomers, will soon retire, imposing an incredible fiscal pressure on the younger generations. The emergence throughout Europe of 'pensioner political parties' and the sheer electoral clout of the baby-boomers make any meaningful redirection of welfare resources towards the younger generations unlikely. Only 15% of young French and 35% of young Germans think their country will be better off in the future than it is now, not to mention the lifetime of austerity facing Greek youth.

The EU's response to this criticism is easily to predict. It will argue that it would love to tackle all these problems that affect the younger generations, but that it does not have the legal competences to do so. Managing the labour market, welfare state, or the housing stock is something that Member States do independently from the EU. Even though this is partially correct (and partially incorrect, as the EU influences these areas heavily through the country-specific recommendations in the European Semester, the excessive deficit procedure, and the austerity programmes), the EU's response is completely beside the point. If the EU wants to sell itself to the young generations, it will need to start selling what those generations *actually want*. If the EU wants to, once again, be the aspirational forum that is embraced by the younger generations as providing an attractive vision of its collective future, it will have to change tack. It will have to stop insisting that limits to roaming charges and the 'seamless use of connected cars' are selling points for the generations pining for a healthier planet, a healthier economy, and a healthier life beyond the market.

The Problems of the New Generations

It is not always easy to distinguish the threats to, and fears of, the younger generations from those of the older ones. Partially this is a problem of data: often the generations are not separated out when asked about these kinds of things. By looking at longer-term trends, however, we can identify at least four types of threats that are particularly acute for the younger generations and their future.

The first long-term threat was discussed in the previous section—and sees to economic stagnation. Even if Europe has never been richer in absolute terms, the distribution of resources has never been more unequal. While the number of billionaires in Europe has been steadily growing over the past years, 26.5% of Europe's under-18s are at risk of poverty and social exclusion. Jobs, housing, and welfare benefits are skewed in favour of the older generations, causing significant exclusion of the younger generations from the elements in life that offer a level of autonomy and independence that previous generations have taken for granted. Higher education has become more expensive in most EU Member States over the past ten years, with the extension of tuition fees or cutting of student grants and family-related benefits. New and precarious employment relationships, including the gig economy and zero-hour contracts, which disproportionately affect younger workers, are making it even more difficult to get by—not to mention the unpaid internships or 'work experience', which is increasingly expected from new entrants on the job market. This increase in competitiveness spills over in a second long-term threat to the new generations.

This second threat is something that many analysts have called the 'delay in life' that is increasingly visible in the youngest generations.

Millennials (and there is no indication that the generations following will be any different) delay their 'rites of passage into adulthood'. Kathleen Shaputis, for example, has found a significant delay in the age at which people move out of their ancestral house, start relationships, get married, or have children.[6] The costs of housing, childcare, education—coupled with the precariousness of work and relative affluence of their parent's generation—mean that younger generations are, in a way, caught in a childhood life. This has led to millennials being called the 'Peter Pan Generation', evoking images of kids trapped in the body of middle age. Beyond the material consequences of this development, more and more data is emerging that suggests that it has significant psychological consequences. Cultural anthropologists argue that these 'rites of passage' are fundamental elements of human growth, which alert fellow citizens as well as the individual of their changing role in society. These rites of passage can be 'secular' or 'sacred', in the words of one of the most famous cultural anthropologists, Arnold van Gennep, and include learning to ride a bike, potty training, first kiss, graduation ceremonies, living alone, getting married, first job, first house, pregnancy, and so on. These moments are important because they signify the transition into another role that comes with different types of responsibility, agency, expectations, membership, and sense of achievement and status. Delaying these transitions—whether because of material scarcity, competitive pressure, or we are too obsessed with our screens and social media profiles—has the potential to lead to disaffection, immaturity, and anxiety. Data presented in early 2018 in Psychological Bulletin confirmed that no generation has ever been so over-medicated, stressed, anxious, and sleep-deprived as millennials.[7] Until the next generation is researched, that is.

The third long-term threat to the younger generations comes from our consumption patterns. First and foremost, this means physical consumption. The World Obesity Federation recently published the 'Obesity Atlas for the European Union', which makes for scary reading. Overall, between 25% and 30% of children are overweight, while the percentage of obesity sits at around 6–13% depending on the Member State (this was 0.2% in 1970!). In Greece, for example, childhood obesity sits at 12%, while the percentage of overweight children is 42%. Both overweight and obese children have a pronouncedly increased chance of having severe psychological or health issues—ranging from hypertension and depression to asthma and diabetes. Obesity has been linked to several types of cancer, and research shows that obese children often struggle their whole lives with their health. Beyond the psychological and physical toll, of course, obesity is also linked to enormous costs for the healthcare system. Obesity is a problem that correlates very pronouncedly with levels of income and education. In simple terms: the poorer and less educated your parents are, the more likely you are to be overweight or obese. While the causes of obesity are clear (too much sugar, too few vegetables, and too little sport), most government tactics to stem the tide of obese children have not yet worked.

The consumption patterns of the younger generations also cause problems in another area. If anything defines the millennials and the generations that follow, it is their access to the internet. This has made us the 'most connected' and 'most flexible' generation yet (as well as the most narcissistic), but also one whose lives are more affected by online threats, ranging from cyberbullying, revenge porn, identity theft, and privacy invasion. The way in which digital consumption affects our safety, privacy, and state of mind has not been researched extensively, but that certain threats of over-consumption (or over-sharing!) exist is clear.

The fourth and final long-term threat for the younger generations has to do with creating a sustainable world. This is most clearly manifested in the fight against climate change. At the rate we are going about it now, the weather forecast for 2050 (when Generation α will be between 25 and 40 years old) is not just 'warmer', but includes—in Europe—lethal heat waves, water shortages, unprecedented storms, flash floods, threats to agricultural practice by increased rainfall and droughts (depending on where you are in Europe), an increase in sea level, the extinction of certain types of plants and animals, and the likelihood of large numbers of environmental refugees. While it seems that we cannot prevent these occurrences by 2050, we *can* influence just how severe they will be. Project Drawdown, for example, has collected 100 ideas on how to resist global warming, ranging from the (obvious) wind turbines and the promotion of emission-free transport to more indirect projects such as fostering female reproductive autonomy or repopulating the mammoth steppes (not with actual mammoths).

There are some indications that awareness of the impact of pollution on our lives and planet is slowly translating into small-scale action. Anne Hidalgo, the Paris major, has closed the banks of the Seine to traffic to prevent pollution. Düsseldorf and Stuttgart are banning diesel cars on certain days, while Paris and Copenhagen are banning all petrol- and diesel fuelled cars altogether by 2030. Cheap, public rental bikes can now be found in most big European cities, while all public transport is free in Tallinn. A shop in Amsterdam opened the first 'plastic-free' shopping aisle, with more expected to open in the coming years. Activists are working hard to make consumers aware of the fact that blueberries in the supermarket in Antwerp actually originate from Chile, and to make them understand what the environmental impact is of a cheeky weekend trip to Barcelona. Needless to say, while these initiatives are certainly praiseworthy, they will not prevent the worst effects of climate change. As discussed, combating climate change in any meaningful sense requires political power and resources to be reallocated at a level beyond the state. Without this reallocation, and significant rethinking of energy, transport and industrial policy, the threat of climate change will become the reality for the younger generations.

THE OPPORTUNITIES FOR THE NEW GENERATIONS

It's not all doom and gloom for the younger generations. They will also be the generations that will most benefit from some exciting technological and societal advances. Any meaningful discussion about the new common purpose of the EU, therefore, must not just look at the threats that can unite Europeans but also at the opportunities that may bind them. The biggest source of these opportunities is technological advances. Millennials and the generations that follow will see dramatic changes in their lifetime in probably all facets of daily life. It is pointless to even begin to speculate on the form and shape of these innovations. But we do not have to be as pessimistic (or is it prophetic?) as the makers of *Black Mirror* to realise that powerful technology, artificial intelligence, and robotics have the potential to change—quite literally—everything: from healthcare to sexuality, from entertainment to death, from war to art, from the way we are born to the way we govern.

With these technological advances comes the question of power and purpose, something that is increasingly discussed in the context of drones, artificial intelligence, and data privacy: what *should* we use the innovations for? As with all innovations—whether it is the steam engine, nuclear fusion, or the internet—they can be used to achieve nefarious, profitable, constructive, or collective ends.

The point of this section is not to predict which technological advances the younger generations will face, or how they ought to engage with the opportunities that these advances offer. The focus here is narrower: there is one sector in which technology *can* be used to make a big difference to the lives of the millennials, and the members of Generations Z and α. That is the workplace. The rise in automation, 3D-printing, artificial intelligence, and robotics will reshape all industries, but particularly the ones that rely on the low-skilled labour. As many experts have highlighted, this wave of automation could lead to apocalyptic inequality, mass unemployment, and a decimated welfare state; but it also could liberate millions of people from their mind-dulling work, serve as a catalyst for a project of radical equality, and allow for a much healthier work-life balance. The younger generations might be the first to experience a life of real freedom, wherein they can decide what to do with their lives free from economic pressures. Or they might be generations trapped in a cycle of competitiveness, unemployment, and a shrinking welfare state for the rest of their lives.

Nick Srnicek and Alex Williams, two academics based in London, have worked on how technology might actually allow us to have some control over our collective future. Their work focuses on the presumption that the advantages that tech provides over the coming decades are such that it would allow us to radically reinvent the way in which we live, by generating vast wealth without the need for an extensive labour force. They estimate that between 47% and 80% of current jobs will be automatable in the next 20 years—and that new processes such as deep learning, big data, and virtual reality will mean that this effect will increasingly be felt in industries that we have long considered to be insulated from automation: journalism, legal clerks, artists, and chefs.[8] The automation of these types of jobs might capture headlines ('robot paints new Rembrandt!'), but these will be dwarfed by the headlines indicating the numbers of workers replaced in factory lines, marketing, entertainment, and government administration. Even in the conservative estimate of an automation rate of 47%, this would mean that 108 million workers become redundant in the EU in the next 20 years. This does not necessarily mean, of course, that fewer jobs will be available. New jobs will emerge, as in any technological revolution, and it is too early to predict if these will outweigh the losses. It is clear, however, that this process will affect the least skilled and least enfranchised workers more than others. It is equally clear that under current conditions, most of the vast wealth generated by automation will end up in the pockets of the owners of the new forms of technology.

Rather than seeing this process of automation as a threat, however, we can also see it as an opportunity. The young generations are uniquely placed to rethink the role of human labour in our economic system. With good policies (and electoral demands), it is not particularly difficult to imagine a world in which automation generates vast wealth without requiring humans to do degrading or meaningless work for 40 hours a week. The movement questioning this assumption is already well-established. In the book *Time is on Our Side*, for example, a group of academics suggests that a 30-hour workweek makes most economic sense.[9] A YouGov poll in 2014 shows a significant majority of British public in favour of a four-day workweek.[10] More radical initiatives, such as the establishment of a universal basic income, would completely liberate individuals from the need to work in order to be able to live a dignified and autonomous life.

What these initiatives have in common is the feeling that we spend too much of our time, energy, and creativity doing things that we do not like; which leaves insufficient time, energy, and creativity to do the things that we actually *want* to do. This is also the feeling that might unite the younger generations and serve as a new collective aspiration: how can we use the incredible potential of new technological developments to create a future that offers us the same standard of living with the addition of the one thing that we all want: time. More time with friends and family, to care for parents and children, to play sports, be creative or—and this is the bottom line—*to do whatever it is that you want to do*. I imagine it's not easy to find people that would walk away from such a future.

CONSTRUCTING THE FUTURE

Let us circle back to the main question in this chapter: how can the EU sell itself to the younger generations? We have seen that this requires a common purpose that offers direction to the integration project and that can enthuse its citizens. We have also discussed possible threats and opportunities that are specific to these younger generations, and that could serve as starting points in the construction of a new common purpose for the EU. But how do we go from one to the other? How can the EU reorient itself around new purposes so that it—once again—is embraced as an aspirational project by the younger generations? This process requires three steps.

First, a new common purpose needs to be identified. The point of this chapter was not to suggest one particular new common purpose or aspiration for the EU. The threats of economic stagnation and climate change, or the opportunity provided by automation *might* be such aspirations, but defining the direction of the integration project is not the task of one person (let alone me). Who, then, is in charge? How are these new ideas and aspirations born?

The answer is that, usually, such ideas emerge quite organically and disparately. The idea for 'peace and prosperity', for example, in 1945, took its inspiration from the *Ventotene Manifesto* written by imprisoned Italian thinkers in the Second World War, from ideas within the French foreign office, but were also based on ideas that link back to Immanuel Kant, Victor Hugo, and the German ordo-liberals. Such ideas are then translated into an imagined collective future by networks of activists, politicians, bureaucrats, lawyers, and ordinary citizens. The work of French political sociologist Antoine Vauchez, for example, shows how the construction of the EU's legal order was to a large extent determined by quite dense networks of transnational academics, entrepreneurs, and Commission officials.

These networks, which the sociologist Charles Tilly calls 'trust networks', operate together to defend and advance a certain cause. This may sound all a bit opaque and conspiracy-like, but is much more banal than you would expect. Trust networks, which typically emerge around a shared purpose or a shared interest, range from traditional political groups such as *Black Lives Matter* to religious groups and from volunteer groups to professional associations or even street gangs. All these groups (or networks) are based on strong ties between the members, and formed around a certain collective aspiration. These are the sites where new ideas are formed, nuanced, solidified, and advanced in the public realm. The beauty of trust networks is that they are difficult to control. As soon as a sufficient number of people feel sufficiently strong about something—whether it is about the position of women in society, the threat of climate change, or the need to protect workers—these trust networks and the associated ideas emerge organically.

The second step, however, is to translate these ideas into policy, into real-world action. Charles Tilly, in his work, calls this the integration of trust networks into a system of rule. What this means, essentially, is that governments will try to co-opt or convince trust networks that the government can help them meet their aspirations. After all, if a government can convince a trust network to cooperate, the government strengthens its own authority or legitimacy. Governments, in other words, remain responsive to what happens on their territory by including trust networks, their claims, passion, and energy *within* the system of rule.

This is something that modern states have become quite good at—think of the way in which they fund religious activities and NGOs, or the way in which the demands of protest groups such as the women's voting movement or the 1968ers have been incorporated in government policy. This is not surprising. To use our branding language once again, governments need to be responsive to the emergence of discontent and trust networks to be able to 'sell' themselves.

You do not need to be a specialist in EU politics to know that, unlike national governments, the EU is particularly bad at doing this. Partially this is because transnational trust networks, that span several states and make collective claims, are only slowly emerging. Partially, however, it is also a problem of the internal structuring of the EU. As we will see in the next chapter, the EU's internal functioning is based on a very rigid understanding of what the EU is *for*. The very nature of the EU—its institutions, voting mechanisms, legal order, and powers—is specifically constructed to attain its original purpose of 'peace and prosperity'. This makes it very difficult for the EU to respond to new ideas, aspirations, or challenges or integrate them in the way that a nation state could (and would).

This leads us to the third step in the translation from a new aspiration into a project that can 'sell' itself to the citizen. For this, we go back to Simon Anholt's work on the way in which countries brand themselves. Having a common purpose or collective aspiration is only the starting point in this process. For a polity to be able to 'sell' itself as being relevant for the attainment of a specific aspiration, it must *actually pursue this aspiration*. This may seem a most obvious statement, but it matters greatly. The research conducted by Anholt suggests that identifying a common purpose without *actually* trying to achieve it—which, basically, makes it an exercise in propaganda or PR—does not fool the citizen.

As we will see in the next chapter, the EU's current structure—from its legal powers, to the division between its institutions, and the rights of the citizens—is perfectly set up to achieve 'peace and prosperity'. And, in fact, the EU generated a whole lot of peace and prosperity over the past 60 years. The EU, in other words, could 'sell' itself for the best part of its history because it, first, sold something that met the collective aspirations of its citizens, and, second, *actually* achieved those aspirations. If the EU wants to convince the younger generations of its continued relevance, then it must not only 'find' a new common purpose but also transform itself internally in the way that is best suited to actually achieve that purpose.

A crucial part of this process of *actually* achieving a certain purpose, of course, lies in good policies. But so-called symbolic policies are equally important. These are particularly remarkable, surprising or poetic policies that, to speak with Anholt, have 'an intrinsic communicative power' and 'are emblematic of the strategy: they are at the same time a component of the national story and the means of telling it'.[11] Examples of such policies are Estonia's declaration of internet access as a human right, as part of its emergence as a forerunner in technological developments; Ireland's referendums on gay marriage and abortion, as part of the economic and social modernisation process; the decision of the major of Florence to ban McDonalds from the city centre, as part of his ambition to protect the cultural identity of the city; or Angela Merkel's dramatic opening of Germany's borders during the refugee crisis, as a signifier of the openness of German society. These symbolic policies matter because they identify an aspiration and simultaneously pursue it.

CONCLUSION

In thinking about its future, the EU must carefully consider how it can 'sell' itself to its younger generations. Simply leaning back on its project of 'peace and prosperity' won't do. This is not to question the EU's success in pursuing that objective—in fact, it is the exact opposite: the EU has made this objective irrelevant by offering its younger generations a peaceful and prosperous continent. If the EU wants to remain relevant for these generations, however, it will need to construct a new common purpose, paying specific attention to the threats and opportunities that are faced by them. And it will need to relentlessly pursue that new common purpose by reforming its internal functioning, rethinking its policies, and displaying some originality in articulating symbolic policies that further its pursuit of the common purpose. This is not a cynical exercise of 'selling' itself to the citizens; it is a project that makes citizens care about the EU, and, perhaps more crucially, *take* care of it.

NOTES

1. S. Anholt, *Places: Identity, Image and Perception* (Palgrave Macmillan, 2010) 104.
2. T. Judt, *Postwar: A History of Europe since 1945* (Penguin, 2011) 6.
3. European Commission, *White Paper on the Future of Europe*, COM (2017) 2025 of 1 March 2017.

4. Bertelsmann Stiftung Policy Brief 2016/01, *What Millennials think about the Future of the EU and the Euro*, available online.

5. Rapporto 2017 della Fondazione Bruno Visentini, '*Il Divario Generazionale tra conflitti e solidarità*', available at: http://www.fondazionebrunovisentini.eu/pubblicazioni/il-divario-generazionale-tra-conflitti-e-solidarieta-generazioni-al-confronto/

6. K. Shaputis, The Crowded Nest Syndrome: Surviving the Return of Adult Children (Clutter Fairy, 2004).

7. T. Curran and A. P. Hill, '*Perfectionism is Increasing Over Time: A Meta-Analysis of Birth Cohort Differences From 1989 to 2016*' (2018) 144 Psychological Bulletin, 1.

8. N. Srnicek and A. Williams, *Inventing the Future: Postcapitalism and a World without Work* (Verso 2016) 86.

9. A. Coote and J. Franklin (eds.), *Time on our side: Why we all need a shorter working week* (NEF 2013).

10. YouGov Poll of 14–15 April 2014. Full results available at http://cdn.yougov.com/cumulus_uploads/document/l7cg9dxpoh/YG-Archive-140415-4-Day-Week.pdf

11. S. Anholt, *Places: Identity, Image and Perception* (Palgrave Macmillan, 2010) 6.

CHAPTER 5

Public

It is hard to imagine that a Czechoslovak band called *The Plastic People of the Universe* was at the start of one of the most original and inspiring movements of rebellion during the Cold War. In 1976, the Czechoslovak authorities decided to crack down on certain members of the so-called underground—a loosely knitted collection of writers, musicians, artists, and their fans, whose political ideals and lifestyle were deemed offensive by the leaders of the Czechoslovak Communist regime. Among others, two members of *The Plastic People of the Universe*—an experimental psychedelic rock band—were arrested and tried for non-conformism and disturbance of the peace. These trials became a catalyst for the establishment of Charter 77. This Charter was a manifesto signed by 242 individuals, including renegade politicians, reformists, intellectuals, and artists. One of its founders and most famous proponents was Václav Havel, who would later serve as president of Czechoslovakia and the Czech Republic between 1989 and 2003.

Charter 77 made a somewhat ironic and counterintuitive demand: it suggested that the Czechoslovak authorities follow their own laws and specifically the Helsinki Accords of 1975 (a pact containing principles linking the western and eastern blocs) in which it promised to respect human rights, including the right to freedom of expression. Charter 77 did not demand the end of the Communist regime, but simply suggested it should obey its own laws a bit better. It is, at the same time, difficult to overstate the radicalism of this demand in the world of today, as much as

F. de Witte, *re:generation Europe*,
https://doi.org/10.1007/978-3-030-19788-9_5

it is difficult to overstate how annoyed the Czechoslovak authorities were by Charter 77. The signatories were subject to yearlong intimidation, harassment, and were marginalised by state-led publicity campaigns.

The story of Charter 77 is, in many ways, a political incarnation of the one of the most influential insights from communication studies in the twentieth century: *the medium is the message*. This phrase, coined by the Canadian academic Marshall McLuhan in the 1960s, is meant to highlight that the *method* through which something is done is inseparable from, and often more expressive than, the *content* that is conveyed.[1] If this sounds very opaque, think of Charter 77. The message of that project was to create a more open society in which freedom of expression was protected for all Czechoslovak citizens. The medium through which this message was most powerfully expressed, then, was through a public intervention—by actually *using* the freedom of expression: the manifesto was not only distributed as widely as possible, including major international news outlets, the Czechoslovak president, and the national assembly, but also distributed with the names of the signatories attached, rather than anonymously (which could have saved the signatories years of persecution). The very open and public nature of the protest and its inevitable response by the authorities were its very point. The medium, clearly, was the message.

If this still sounds opaque, think of the EU. The EU is also fundamentally geared around this insight. As we saw in the previous chapter, the internal functioning of the EU—from the tasks of the European Commission to the rules on free movement, and from the role of national courts to the rules on cucumbers—fundamentally revolves around the attainment of its central message: peace and prosperity. The medium (i.e., the institutional machinery of European integration) *is* the message. This has made the project of European integration wildly successful: it has attained more peace and prosperity than could ever have been imagined in 1957. But it is also a problem for the EU. Now that the commitment to peace and prosperity seems to generate less and less enthusiasm in Europe's citizens, the EU has started to look elsewhere for a new message. The problem is that it is stuck with the same medium: the institutional configuration of the EU has hardly changed at all.

The problem that such a fundamental mismatch leads to is already alluded to by Havel in the essay 'The Power of the Powerless'. He argues that at the centre of the Communist regime was a paradox—a mismatch between its medium and its message, if you will. Havel uses the example of a greengrocer to drive this point home. The greengrocer is sent a sign that says '*Workers of the World, Unite!*' that he is asked to display in the shop window. Does the greengrocer actually think that the workers of the world should unite? It's difficult to tell, after all, given that everyone knows that the greengrocer will be relieved of his job (as well as his apartment, holiday in Bulgaria, and children's education) if he chooses *not* to display the sign. What Havel suggests, among other things, is that popular support is difficult to gauge under an ideological straightjacket. Simply observing the greengrocer and his shop window does not tell us much about the greengrocers' commitment to the Communist regime—at best it tells us that he is committed to keeping up appearances. This blindspot is often a problem for regimes with strong ideological or authoritarian tendencies: it is difficult to see who means it when all citizens are instructed on penalty of death to wave flags.

The EU suffers a similar paradox. Its commitment to peace and prosperity is so deeply engrained in everything that the EU does that it has never even occurred to politicians to ask the citizen if they still agree to it. How is it possible, otherwise, that Brexit took everyone by surprise? How is it possible that 52% of the electorate of a Member State rejected the values of openness, free movement, cooperation, and economic liberalisation that the EU has stood for since 1957? Look at the worried reactions of politicians in the other Member States after Brexit—falling over each other to shout that the EU's purpose had to be reformed to become more 'of' the citizens and 'for' the citizens. What does this tell us? It tells us, above all else, that a change in the EU's *medium* is much more important than a change to its message. Only by reorganising itself internally so that its rules and institutions are open to the citizens' voices will the EU *actually* be able to change its message. This chapter discussed the kind of radical reconfiguration that is required for this to take place.

THE EU'S UNDEMOCRATIC DNA

In his essay 'The Power of the Powerless', Havel argues that a political system almost inevitably creates dissenters whenever it is insufficiently flexible to respond to new demands of its people. As he puts it, in the first page of his essay, 'the system has become so ossified politically that there is practically no way for non-conformity to be implemented within its official structures'.[2] The problem that Havel identifies is one that the EU is also faced with. Properly understood, however, the problem is not that the EU's citizens have 'non-conformist' or dissenting opinions (although many might). The real problem is that the EU is incapable of listening to those opinions.

This problem is relatively new. For a long time, the EU's unresponsiveness to the citizen has been the *very point* of the EU. The purpose of the integration project has always been to secure 'peace and prosperity' after the Second World War. The instrument for achieving this has been to ossify the political system—that is, to make sure that no one could alter that central objective or stand in the way of its achievement. This has been done in a number of ways.

Let's start with the institutions of the European Union. The reason why the EU is unlike national political systems, where a government and parliament share power (the latter usually electing and controlling the former), is that the EU is fundamentally organised around reconciling different interests. The Council represents the national interest of the Member States; the European Parliament represents the interests of the European citizenry; and the European Commission represents the collective European interest, the 'common good'. None of these institutions can pass a law all by itself. They are condemned to cooperate with each other, which, in theory, results in the decisions being acceptable for all three interest groups: it is acceptable for the Member States, for the European Parliament, and serves the European common good.

The purpose of this convoluted process, in which all interests must be safeguarded, is that this makes sure that the EU is seen as legitimate: that its decisions are accepted by all participants to the integration process. It also means, however, that laws are incredibly difficult to change. If we would want to change, for example, Article 7 of Directive 2013/29, which lays down age restrictions for the sale of fireworks, we would need the following political support: the Commission must think that a change is in the interest of the EU as a whole, the European Parliament must support the measure with a majority of 50% + 1 vote, and the ministers in the Council must support it—roughly, depending on population numbers of the individual Member States—with a two-third majority. This is an incredibly high threshold. In most Member States, you would need a less significant majority to change the constitution or even the name of the country! So whereas the convoluted decision-making process in the EU serves to make sure that its decisions are acceptable to a large number of stakeholders, it also means that such rules are difficult to agree on or change. This, as the German political scientist Fritz Scharpf has highlighted, means that the EU contains a strong *status quo* bias—which makes it particularly unresponsive to new arguments and political claims made by citizens.

The same logic can be found in the EU's legal system, which is centrally premised on the idea of supremacy—which means that when a national law and a European law conflict, the latter always wins. This makes it impossible for national governments or parliaments to suspend the application of EU law, or to contest it by adopting contradictory laws. Rights that citizens derive from EU law, such as the right to move freely across borders, cannot be stopped by political actors on the national level. It is the responsibility of national courts to prevent national decision-makers from doing so, which means that it has become *legally impossible* for national politicians to contest or challenge EU rules by adopting alternative norms.

This problem is made worse by another *status quo* bias in the system. The EU Treaties do not, like most constitutional documents, only lay down the division of powers and fundamental rights. Instead, they regulate in great detail the political orientation of many of the policy areas in which the EU has a say. This ranges from monetary policy, rules on equality, rules on the mobility of people, and industrial policy. Changing these rules laid down in the Treaty requires an eye-watering majority: all Member States *and* all national parliaments have to vote in favour of any change. This means that 51% of the Maltese parliament, representing roughly 220,000 citizens, has the power to block what 511,280,000 citizens may want. Or, to put it even more starkly, the rules on Treaty revision offer the possibility for 0.04% of the EU's population to block what 99.96% may want.

While all these rules serve the explicit purpose of safeguarding the attainment of the EU's message of 'peace and prosperity' by making it impossible to challenge that objective, it also makes the EU incredibly unresponsive to what the citizens want from it *beyond* that objective. In other words, even if the EU would want to listen to its citizens, its internal rules make that close to impossible.

From the start of the integration process until the early 1990s, this ossification of the EU was not considered to be problematic. Everyone agreed on the objective of 'peace and prosperity', after all. Since the 1990s, however, the contestation of the EU has grown stronger ever year. For some, the EU is too neo-liberal. For others, it is too socially minded. For some, the EU is too generous towards states that need to be bailed out. For others, the EU is much too harsh in its austerity demands. For some, it is too strong on enforcing fundamental rights in the Member States, while for others it is too weak. For some, the EU is undermining the welfare state through its rules on free movement, while for others it fails to express a minimum level of solidarity between citizens. This list is endless—every single policy of the EU is contested *somewhere* in the EU, and often from contradictory positions at the same time. This contestation, as such, is *not* a problem. In fact, the EU is missing a trick here: contestation has the potential to make the EU responsive to discontent and dissent; it has the potential to bring some passion, engagement, and emotion from its citizens; and it has the potential for the EU to secure more acceptance for its rules. Contestation, as Havel had already highlighted, is only a problem when the political system does not have a place for it, and cannot institutionalise it.

For the EU, this problem is manifesting itself in the past years with alarming speed and has become the most pressing challenge for its long-term survival. As we have seen with Brexit, the impossibility to contest the policy orientation of the EU means that the EU has become a binary choice for its citizens: you are either in favour of *this* EU, or against it. Being in favour of *another kind of EU*—one that is more social, or has more austerity—is not a plausible political position. The institutional ossification is such that not a single national politician, not even the German chancellor, can promise voters that they will change the EU in a particular direction. This dynamic, as we saw in the first chapter, also offers an explanation for the rise of Eurosceptic parties, both on the left and on the right: they are the only ones that offer voters the mechanism for meaningful political change: leaving the EU and its ossified pursuit of 'peace and prosperity' altogether. Obviously, this narrative is much too simplistic, as the Brexiteers have found out, but it should serve as a warning sign (with five exclamation marks) for the EU about its future: if it does not somehow internalise the citizens' opinions, contestation will only increase in force and scope.

ENTER THE PUBLIC

How can we open up the EU for the public? How can we reconfigure the system so that its new guiding logic is no longer 'peace and prosperity' but simply being responsive to what citizens want from it? The answer comes in three steps: it requires legal changes, institutional innovations, and the creation of a European public. Only by such a radical transformation of the *medium* of integration can the EU's message change.

The most basic precondition for such a Europe is that the public must be able to *actually change* the direction of European integration. This may sound like an obvious truth, but—as we have seen in the previous sections—the current set-up of the EU does not allow for this. The inability of citizens to change the direction of European integration is exactly the reason why so few citizens, in fact, engage at all. Even *if* citizens were to become active, organised, and demand that the EU act on a certain matter, they might (justifiably) feel as if no one is listening.

The first step that is needed to make the EU more public, then, is a juridical one: we need to rewrite the Treaties and make sure that the EU's objectives and its policy choices are 'up for grabs', that is, are tailored to what citizens actually want from the EU. This means that the Treaty will look more like national constitutions do: it will lay down the powers of the different institutions as well as the ground rules for equal and free participation of all citizens in the integration process. Whether we should have a liberal or conservative policy on free movement, or whether we prefer more or less solidarity in the Euro-zone and with refugees, on the other hand, are questions to be answered by the European public, not laid down in stone by the Treaties.

The second step in making sure that the public becomes engaged with Europe's future is institutional. As we saw, the current institutional configuration is very complex—laws are adopted by three different institutions. That configuration worked very well when the integration project was about pursuing 'peace and prosperity'. But if we want to move to an EU that is responsive to what citizens want from it, it will need to change its institutions as well. Of course, there is a very simply blueprint available for making the EU more sensitive to its public. And that is the blueprint of the nation state, where citizens elect the parliament, and a majority in parliament forms the government. In this way, there is a clear link between what the citizens want and the policy direction taken by the government. If the government does something that a majority of parliament disapproves of, after all, parliament can simply sack the government. This direct link of accountability and political control is indispensable for an EU that is responsive to its public, and where the public has the feeling that they can *actually* influence the direction and nature of European integration.

A move to such a parliamentary system requires changes to the way in which European elections are held. At the moment, elections for the European Parliament are based on national lists: citizens vote for the same parties that they vote for in national elections. This has led, as many commentators have highlighted, to EP elections being 'second order national elections'. Voters typically vote with national politics in mind—after all, they are voting on national parties—and not with European politics in mind. In other words, even if we are voting for the European Parliament elections, we are not really choosing *what kind* of EU we want.

The only way to make European elections a contest of the kind of EU the public wants is to establish transnational party lists, each with their own vision and agenda for the integration project, and each with their own candidate for the presidency of the European government. This would mean that Europeans, when they go to the ballot box, choose not between national parties but between alternative visions of Europe: alternative ways of solving the refugee crisis; alternative ways of dealing with the Euro-zone; and alternative ways of responding to Brexit. A Romanian, Italian, or Danish citizen would have to decide what kind of Europe they want, and then each would cast a vote accordingly: for the European Greens, the European Liberals, Socialists, Conservatives, Christian-Democrats, or Eurosceptics. Each party would present and defend their own views, criticise the other party programmes, seek media attention, field charismatic leaders, and—generally—act the way in which we intuitively expect electoral competition to function.

These institutional changes would allow us to understand what Europeans actually want from the integration project, and would allow to EU to be responsive to those demands. It would also galvanise citizen engagement with the EU. Once the questions that affect all of us—from free movement to the future of the Euro; from the refugee crisis to trade deals with the United States—are answered by us rather than removed from us, citizens are much more likely to engage. The move towards a parliamentary system also means transforming the European Commission into a government that is directly responsive and accountable to the European Parliament, and transforming the Council into an upper chamber with much more limited powers.

The third and final precondition in the transformation of the EU's is a step that the EU cannot make itself. Once the EU has reconfigured itself so that it can listen to its public, it needs that public to actually say something. The creation of a European public—whereby Europeans come together, voice their needs and desires, and attempt to influence the future of the EU—is to a large extent dependent on something called 'cleavages'. Cleavages, essentially, are central divides in society, which structure politics and allow citizens to make sense of complex political questions. They are, in a sense, intermediary political structures that bridge the gap between the public and government. The traditional cleavages that have structured political conflict in the last century are the opposition between church-state views of society, between urban-rural communities, centre-periphery interests, or owner–worker preferences. These are, in other words, the central elements of conflict around which political discussions and voter preferences have crystallised. The EU needs these cleavages: they set a certain logic and predictability to political contestation, allow citizens to engage, and create the institutional sophistication required for effective governance. This type of conflictual opposition of views clearly already exists in the EU. The 'solution' for the Euro-zone crisis, for example, creates evident conflict between the younger and older generations and between banks and pensioners. Brexit highlights a clear cleavage between citizens open to globalisation and those opposed to its dislocating social and economic effects. The refugee crisis shows a divide between those in favour of more solidarity with the vulnerable migrant and those in favour of stronger protection of the EU's borders. All these cleavages already exist within the political systems of the Member States, but have not yet emerged transnationally in the EU.

How can we translate these political tensions into transnational parties, interest groups, and networks? How, in a sense, can we create a European public? Here the work of Charles Tilly is very insightful. His work has focused on something called 'trust networks'. These are groups of people that have organised themselves to defend a particular interest, value, or 'way of living'. These trust networks can facilitate the creation of cleavages and serve as intermediary structures between the government and the public. The reason for this is that governments are interested in incorporating trust networks within government. The more these trust networks can be convinced to become part of the state, after all, the easier the state can govern society—because larger (parts of) the public have a stake in the state's survival.

Tilly shows that the most effective way of incorporating trust networks into government is through democracy: it makes trust networks commit to the authority of the state because they know that they'll have a chance to rule and impose their preferred policy outcomes. As long as these trust networks convince sufficient people of their views, after all, they will be able to implement their views. This method of democratic decision-making also makes sure that trust networks remain committed to the state when they *lose* elections: next time round, after all, they might win. Trust networks, in other words, tend to participate in democratic rule not when they agree with all the outcomes that it produces, but when they believe in the *system*. By opening up the direction of integration to whatever the European public wants, then, the EU will create its public as if by magic. But institutional changes must come *before* such a public will emerge.

These three changes to the EU's 'medium'—sketched only very briefly here—will allow the EU to transform its message into something that centres on the citizen, rather than on functional objectives.

WHO IS EUROPE'S PUBLIC?

The biggest obstacle in creating a European public is, perhaps counterintuitively, the Member State. Under the changes proposed above, Member States stand to lose a lot of power. The reconfiguration of political structures on the level beyond the state means that these states lose their control over the process of integration. At the moment, Malta, or even a simple majority in Maltese parliament, can block Treaty changes that all other European citizens and states may want. This can be seen as an affront to democracy, as a mistake in the EU's architecture: how is it possible that 0.04% of the electorate can potentially stop what 99.96% want? While these rules might have made sense to prevent backsliding and protect the pursuit of 'peace and prosperity', surely they have no place in a Europe that listens to its citizens?

Others, however, see national vetoes as a way to *defend* the citizens' influence over the integration process. For these people, the only way to protect democratic processes is on the national level: why would a majority of the Maltese parliament, which was elected democratically, not be allowed to voice its opinions? Why should we allow a majority of Belgians, Lithuanians, and Hungarians to overrule Maltese citizens?

What underlies this intuition is the idea that democracies require certain properties—such as a common language, thick public spheres, shared historical institutions, and a *demos*, that is, a pre-existing community of people that share a certain ethnic or historical identity. These properties can only be found on the national level, the argument goes, and any attempt to *decrease* the influence of nation states is, therefore, inherently *un*democratic. In other words, a majority of the Maltese parliament—even if it is outvoted by 99.96% of Europe's public—should be allowed to block collective decisions because this is the only way to protect the interests of the Maltese citizens within the EU. Any move towards the creation of a

Europe that focuses on the wishes of its public, rather than on functional objectives agreed among the Member States, then, is actually *un*democratic.

This line of reasoning essentially suggests that the creation of a European public should not go to the detriment of the already existing national publics. While this argument is increasingly gaining traction within both academic and political circles, it is based on two false assumptions. The first false assumption is that, somehow, protecting democracy on the national level is necessary to protect the capacity of citizens to make democratic decisions about their own society. As we saw in the first chapter, we cannot simultaneously have austerity *and* no austerity. In complex situations of interdependence between states, the democratic decisions of some Member States *cannot* be upheld. And we know this, because we have seen it happen: the '*oxi*' referendum in Greece that rejected austerity or the Dutch referendum that rejected the EU-Ukraine Treaty both had no impact on the EU's final decision whatsoever.

Reducing complex questions such as the balance between austerity and solidarity to the tallying of Member States (Finland, Germany, and the Netherlands are in favour, while Greece, Italy, and Portugal are against) misses the point completely. In each of these Member States, some citizens will be in favour of austerity, and some will be against austerity; just as there will be a split on questions of the treatment of refugees or the future of the welfare state. These divisions exist in every single democracy. The European way of making collective decisions, however—by pretending that all Greeks are against austerity and all Germans in favour—obscures these nuances completely. Only by creating a European public that transcends the nation state can such choices be made in a way that actually corresponds to the views of the majority of citizens. Giving power to national publics might *feel* democratic, but the link between national preferences and the final outcome in Brussels is far too tenuous to speak of citizens being able to control their own societies.

The second false assumption that underlies the argument that the voice of national publics needs to be insulated in the EU for the EU to be democratic is that something like a 'national interest' even exists in the first place. This argument presumes that interests are somehow irreducibly linked to nationality: that a Dane living in Copenhagen and a Swede living across a bridge in Malmö somehow have radically different lives, needs, and desires. I spent most of my childhood in Maastricht, a town in the south of the Netherlands, that has—historically—been part of the Roman Empire, part of Charlemagne's territory, was conquered by the Spanish and by Napoleon, formed part of the United Kingdom of the Netherlands, and was, when Belgium gained independence from the Netherlands, a heavily disputed town. Ultimately it was decided that Maastricht was to belong to the Netherlands, which explains the odd appendix that (Dutch) Limburg is on the map of the Netherlands. Two provinces of the Netherlands—Limburg and Brabant—historically have always formed regions with two provinces that are currently in Belgium. As someone who grew up in Maastricht, I was much closer both geographically and in terms of mentality and outlook on life to someone living in Aachen or Genk than to someone living in Amsterdam or Groningen. The habits, temperament, architecture, customs, and food of Maastricht were formed long before the current artificial boundaries of the Netherlands were drawn. The Maastricht dialect is closer to modern-day German than to modern-day Dutch. People living in Maastricht cross the border into Belgium on a weekly basis—whether to buy sandwiches on Sunday morning, to go to the cinema, to get cheaper gasoline, or accidentally while going for an afternoon stroll.

What *national* interests would someone living in Maastricht have with someone in Amsterdam or Groningen, which is not shared with a Belgian living 15 minutes up the road? Which interests are *not* shared with citizens living 10 kilometres to the west or south, but *are* shared with citizens 340 kilometres to the north? To the extent that we share certain interests with fellow nationals, surely those interests transcend the nation state? Surely we all—regardless of borders—have an interest in being able to live a dignified life in a clean environment, with access to jobs and hospitals, and with safe food? There is nothing particularly *national* about these interests.

The Austrian author Robert Menasse makes a similar point when he highlights that someone living in Vienna is much closer in temperament to someone in Bratislava or Sopron, just across the border in Slovakia or Hungary, than to someone in Klagenfurt, which lies 650 kilometres to the west. The same point, of course, can be made by someone living in Bolzano or Biarritz. All European citizens have interests that they want to protect, and values that they cherish. But thinking that these interests are somehow *national*, and that therefore only *national* institutions, and national publics, can defend them, is a dangerous fallacy.

In the EU of today, then, it is the insistence that Member States somehow offer a good way of protecting our democratic way of life that actually *prevents* the EU from being democratic. If we want to change the EU's message—and become more sensitive to what its public wants—we must find ways of redirecting political claims about what our interests are to the level beyond the state.

LONG LIVE THE NATION, OR LONG LIVE THE STATE?

The above section leaves us in a somewhat awkward situation. On the one hand, Europe is fundamentally and unambiguously based on regional diversity—in temperament, humour, breakfast, and fashion sense. All the places where Europeans meet, where they go to school and work, and where they go on holiday or meet friends, are imbued with a strong sense of local identity. This diversity—as we saw in Chap. 2—is the great strength of Europe. On the other hand, Member States are clearly not the best structure through which to decide questions that touch us collectively.

But why does any proposal to create a European public to replace the national ones, or that puts the citizen, instead of the Member States, at the centre of the project of European integration feel so subversive and revolutionary? Why does it engender resistance in most people—including the citizens themselves? Why are we so attached to the nation state?

It seems to me that the nation state reflects at least two things that people care strongly about. The first is a sense of home, or a 'way of doing things'. There is something about the nation state—the food, the greetings, the sounds of the language, the gait, clothing, and temperament of the locals— that simply feels 'right', it feels like home, like something that is safe and ought to be protected. Robert Menasse is highly evocative in capturing this:

> home is where the scents and cadences strike a particular chord; the concrete place where one isn't a visitor, where linguistic peculiarities and idiosyncratic traditions don't necessarily imply affirmation but surely a sense of affiliation. Home is the only place where what's diffuse and obscure becomes clear and concrete, where the bread tastes especially good, where emotions are greater and the anger over small-mindedness is as great as the love of expansive thought.[3]

Home is, at its most basic, a way of doing things—one that is influenced by geography, by history, by the climate and agriculture. This local 'way of doing things' gives structure to our day: from the way we have breakfast, our transport to work, the starting time of and lunch routine at work, the way we treat our children and parents, to evening entertainment and the way our houses look. At a glimpse, most Europeans can tell which dinner scene, living room, or bakery belongs in Copenhagen and which one in Sevilla.

This sense of home is a basic human instinct. It is, however, not necessarily a *national* one. As many authors, including Robert Menasse and Ulrike Guérot, have highlighted, European identity is ultimately a *regional* one. Until its most recent history, Europe has been a patchwork of regions, stretching to the four corners of the EU: from Galicia and Moravia to Scotland, Auvergne, or Transylvania. All the elements that make up 'home'—its sounds, the geography, the food, the humour, or temperament—are ultimately regional. Just think of the regional stereotypes in your own country: radically different traits are subscribed to people from different regions, even in tiny countries like Belgium. The nation state is a relatively recent invention—which artificially threw together different regions and paved over differences by insisting on a single language, a single welfare system, and inventing a shared cultural narrative. It is regional identity, not national identity, and regional 'ways of doing things' that we encounter when we travel through Europe. The life of a person living in the Dolomiti is obviously more similar to that of someone on the other side of the Alps than to that of a factory worker in Sicily—just as a Corsican is temperamentally closer to someone from Sardinia than someone from Paris.

A commitment to protect diversity in Europe and to maintain the hundreds of different 'ways of doing things' is, then, not dependent on the existence of the *nation* state. In fact, as the many regional secession movements across the EU indicate, nation states might actually *prevent* regional diversity and endanger people's sense of what 'home' means to them.

The second reason why we may intuitively be so attached to the idea of the nation state, and become nervous about replacing it with a European public is that the nation state offers the institutional machinery that allows us to *do* certain things. The nation state offers us services, such as trains or postal networks; it provides certain indispensible public goods, such as hospitals, schools, and welfare support for the vulnerable; and it provides us, more generally, with the infrastructure of democracy that allows us to decide on things together in a free and open fashion. What this suggests is that, in fact, our intuitive attachment is to the nation *state*, and not the *nation* state. Historically, there is something to be said for this. The creation of train and road networks helped the state to consolidate its territory, by linking regions together for the purposes of trade and internal migration. The creation of the welfare state was a deliberate attempt to convince citizens of the merits of the state; just as the creation of democratic institutions served to strengthen the authority of rule throughout the territory of the state.

If this is the reason we care so much about the current Member States, there is, of course, no particular reason why we ought to be suspicious of the creation of a European public beyond the state. The fact that certain things are organised on the national level is just historically contingent—it might as well be taken care of (perhaps even better) on a local, regional, transnational, or global level. Nothing about trains, the building of schools, or the running of elections is intrinsically and inextricably tied to the *nation*. And so, revolutionary as it may sound, creating a European public that decides on collective questions beyond the state neither endangers our sense of home, our ability to protect our interests, nor our capacity to take trains, build schools, or engage in democratic decision-making. Quite the opposite, in fact.

However, the only way to make this leap is by pushing for radical changes to the way we 'do' integration. This should come as no surprise by now: the radical transformation of the EU's message (from 'peace and prosperity' to one that centres around its public) must necessarily be matched by an equally radical transformation of the EU's internal configuration.

A RADICAL MEDIUM FOR A PUBLIC MESSAGE

One of the most recognisable brands in Europe is that of Heineken. The man who was for a large extent responsible for its rise in the second half of the twentieth century was called Freddy Heineken. Freddy Heineken had many interests beyond the selling of lager. He was vice-president of the Corviglia Ski Club in Sankt Moritz; he produced a movie called *Als twee druppels water*—in which he also had a cameo—and became a celebrity due to the unfortunate fact that he was kidnapped by a group of criminals in 1983.

Freddy Heineken was also a history buff and set up the *Amsterdam Foundation for Historical Science*. One of the projects that this foundation commissioned, in 1992, had to do with the future of Europe and was called *Eurotopia*. As the title suggests, it offered a bold and innovative vision of the future of Europe. Interestingly, it seems to have foreseen the problems that the integration project would run up against decades later. The *Eurotopia* proposal combines historical and contemporary challenges of European integration in a way that creates a European public while protecting regional differences. It is, in a nutshell, an example of the radical transformation that the EU's internal structure needs so that it can express its new message.

Heineken's proposal sees a radical redrawing of the internal boundaries of Europe. The map, which is reproduced at the end of this chapter,[4] shows a Europe composed of 75 regions of more or less the same amount of inhabitants—between 5 and 12 million inhabitants. The new boundaries are drawn taking account of history, ethnicity, language, and culture. This leads to some modern-day states 'surviving' almost intact, such as Sweden or Norway; and some historical regions being reinstated, such as Catalonia, Alsace, Moravia, Scotland, or Saxony. For the sake of curiosity, I have appended the list of 75 regions (and their capitals) at the end of this chapter.

The point of the *Eurotopia* exercise, of course, is not simply to randomly chop up the different Member States of the EU. The point is to visualise what a radical democratic reconfiguration of Europe would look like.

Heineken's proposal does two things that seem impossible to achieve at the same time. On the one hand, it safeguards our capacity to defend regional diversity, to run efficient welfare states and democracies while, on the other hand, allowing for democratic decision-making on questions that affect the whole of Europe. Let me take these points in turn.

How does the Heineken proposal protect regional identity and the efficiency of the welfare state and democratic participation? As repeatedly highlighted in this book, the cultural identity of Europeans is primarily a *regional* one, not a national one. Someone from Biarritz is closer in temperament, appearance, and culinary preferences to someone in Bilbao than to someone in Paris. The human instinct to protect the qualities, customs, and rituals that are considered to be part of what 'home' is, matters. And the risk of standardisation of social life by homogenising or centralising political, social, or cultural practices must be taken seriously. Defending these values through the institutions on the regional, rather than the national level, then, is a lot more coherent: it allows for the cultivation, articulation, and defence of what 'home' is in a much more ambitious fashion.

The same goes for the creation and delivery of certain collective endeavours, such as the welfare state or democratic institutions. Research shows that these endeavours are provided best in regions that cover between 6 and 12 million inhabitants.[5] This population size is large enough for a sufficient tax base to allow large-scale investments; while it is small enough so that services such as education or healthcare can be tailored to the specific needs of the citizens. Political institutions, moreover, would remain both much more accessible to citizens and accountable to the public than in states with larger populations. As the size of democracies grows, after all, the chances for participation and citizen engagement decrease. A survey that ranks Member States in terms of the delivery of their public goods, the transparency of their decision-making, and public access to the political institutions has seen—for decades now—states with population sizes between 6 and 12 million rank the highest. Creating regions throughout Europe of this size, then, would not simply allow for a more democratic Europe, it would also make for more democratic and efficient *regions*.

Heineken's proposal, however, is not only an ambitious reimagination of regionalism, it is also ambitious in creating a European public. As we have seen in this chapter, the central problem in the current functioning of the EU is that states retain too much power over the way in which decisions are made, to the detriment of the European public. This leads to a very tenuous link between the preferences of the European public and the eventual policy outcomes. This asymmetry would be remedied in Heineken's proposal: a governing system of 75 regions, all with a similar population size, simply cannot offer a veto to *all* regions, nor will it privilege certain more populous or rich regions (as currently happens with Germany and France). Instead, the 75 regions will all have equal power in decision-making in the EU. One could imagine, for example, a bi-cameral parliamentary system, wherein the lower chamber is directly elected by all Europeans, on the basis of transnational party lists, and the upper chamber holds two representatives from each region—elected through regional elections and representing the regional interests. Such a system would not only allow for collective decisions to be made by the European public, but also represent regional interests in a fashion that is much more constructive than the current model.

All this is not to say that the *only* way for the EU to transform itself into a project that centres on the citizen is to follow Heineken's proposal. The discussion of his proposal is merely an example to drive home the radicalism that is involved in resolving the EU's paradox and realigning its medium with its message.

Conclusion

This chapter has argued that the future of the project of European integration depends not just on radically transforming its objective, but on an equally radical transformation of its internal structures. Currently, as we have seen, the EU is unresponsive to what its citizens want from it. And this lack of responsiveness is deliberate: it was considered necessary in order to allow the EU—from its inception in 1957—to achieve its objectives of 'peace and prosperity'.

Now that the EU is in search of a new aspirational project around which its citizens can rally, this lack of responsiveness is becoming problematic. It stands in the way of citizens making use of the integration project to articulate what they think the EU *should* be about.

We stated this chapter with the story of Václav Havel and Charter 77. Their story is highly instructive for the future of the project of European integration in so far as it reveals to what extent the EU's capacity to attain any new objective is tied up with how it organises itself internally. If the EU wants to allow the European public to guide the search of a new collective ambition, it must first *create* this public—which requires a radical reimagination of how the EU is structured, and requires opening up spaces where regional differences and European-wide decision-making coalesce.

And while I am well aware of how mad, impossible, and utopian all this sounds, it is of comfort to imagine what Havel's contemporaries will have made of Charter 77.

Annex: *Eurotopia*'s 75 European Regions and Their Capitals

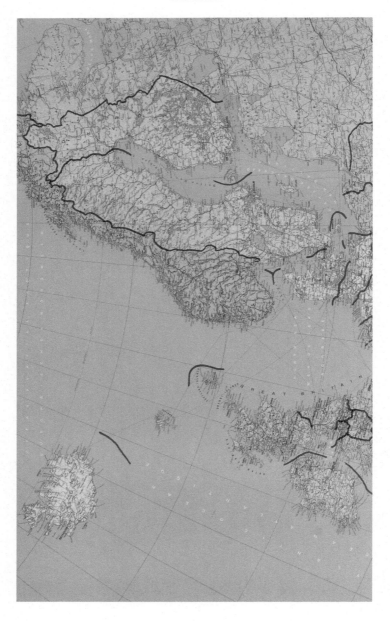

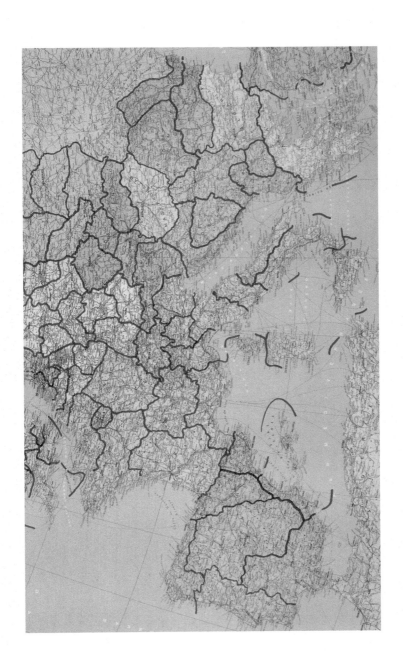

1. Iceland (Reykjavik)
2. Norway (Oslo)
3. Sweden (Stockholm)
4. Finland (Helsinki)
5. Denmark (Copenhagen)
6. Scotland (Edinburgh)
7. Ireland (Dublin)
8. Northumbria (York)
9. Lancaster (Manchester)
10. Wales (Cardiff)
11. Mercia (Birmingham)
12. East-Anglia (Cambridge)
13. London (London)
14. Wessex (Plymouth)
15. Kent (Southampton)
16. Holland–Zeeland (The Hague)
17. Ysselland (Arnhem)
18. Flanders (Brussels)
19. Hainaut (Lille)
20. Schleswig-Holstein (Hamburg)
21. Hannover (Bremen)
22. Brandenburg (Berlin)
23. Saxony (Dresden)
24. Westphalia (Münster)
25. North-Rhineland (Düsseldorf)
26. Thuringia (Erfurt)
27. Rhine-Mosselland (Mainz)
28. Frankenland (Nuremberg)
29. Bavaria (München)
30. Baden-Württemberg (Stuttgart)
31. Poznan (Poznan)
32. Silesia (Wroclaw)
33. Gdansk (Gdansk)
34. Warszawa (Warszawa)
35. Galicia (Krakow)
36. Bohemia (Prague)
37. Moravia (Brno)
38. Slovakia (Bratislava)
39. Austria (Vienna)

40. Noricum (Graz)
41. Picardy-Normandy (Rouen)
42. Ile-de-France (Paris)
43. Burgundy (Nancy)
44. Neustria (Nantes)
45. Aquitania (Bordeaux)
46. Auvergne (Lyon)
47. Provence (Marseille)
48. Galicia-Asturias (Santiago de Compostela)
49. Castilla (Madrid)
50. Navarre-Aragon (Bilbao)
51. Catalonia (Barcelona)
52. Valencia (Valencia)
53. Andalusia (Sevilla)
54. Portugal (Lisbon)
55. Switzerland (Bern)
56. Piedmont (Torino)
57. Lombardy (Milan)
58. Venice (Venice)
59. Tuscany (Bologna)
60. Umbria (Rome)
61. Apulia (Bari)
62. Naples (Naples)
63. Sicily (Palermo)
64. Hungary (Budapest)
65. Croatia (Croatia)
66. Bosnia-Herzegovina (Sarajevo)
67. Serbia (Belgrade)
68. Albania (Tirana)
69. Transylvania (Cluj-Napoca)
70. Moldavia (Bacau)
71. Wallachia (Bucharest)
72. Bulgaria (Sofia)
73. Skopje (Skopje)
74. Greece (Athens)
75. Cyprus (Nicosia)

NOTES

1. M. McLuhan, *Understanding Media: The Extensions of Man* (McGraw-Hill, 1964).
2. V. Havel, *Power of the Powerless* (Routledge, 1985) 23.
3. R. Menasse, *Engaged Citizens, European Peace and Democratic Deficits* (Seagull Press, 2016) 89.
4. A. H. Heineken, *The United States of Europe* (*A Eurotopia?*) (De Amsterdamse Stichting voor de Historische Wetenschap, 1992).
5. The traditional references here are C. Northcote Parkinson, *The Law of Delay* (Mass Market, 1970) and L. Kohr, *The Breakdown of Nations* (Routledge, 1986). A more recent restatement is A. Alesina and E. Spolaora, *The Size of Nations* (MIT Press, 2005).

CHAPTER 6

Ten Policy Ideas for *re:generation Europe*

This chapter makes ten concrete suggestions on how the EU can make use of the trust between its citizens, create new collective aspirations that its younger generations can rally around, and become more sensitive to the claims made by its public. As elaborated in the previous chapters, these three ideas—trust, aspirations, and public—are indispensible in the evolution of the EU into a project that is ready for the next 50 years, and for the challenges and opportunities that the coming decades will bring. The proposals that follow in this chapter try to work through some of the insights of the previous chapters and see how we can give a real-world meaning to those ideas. How can we foster trust between Europeans? Which new ideas might serve as a common aspiration that all Europeans can rally around? Which changes can be made to create a European public that is more engaged with the integration process?

On the outset, it should be made clear that the ten policy proposals that follow are not meant as a checklist for saving the EU. The purpose of these proposals is to show that the EU does not *need* to be about the efficient creation of an internal market or about making citizens' lives easier. It can also be more whimsical, symbolic, and innovative. The EU can be more playful, and more geared towards creating a kind of society that represents Europe: one that is about a good work-life balance, about sustainable consumption, and about respect for difference. These are not proposals that 'fix' the EU, but that could serve to lay the foundations for the creation of a Europe as described in the previous chapters.

© The Author(s) 2020
F. de Witte, *re:generation Europe*,
https://doi.org/10.1007/978-3-030-19788-9_6

The following proposals range from the scandalously ambitious to the mundane. Most are—at the moment—politically improbable, legally impossible, and far-fetched. But that is not a problem. The problem lies in presuming that the EU cannot evolve—politically, legally, or culturally— and that the current *status quo* will be maintained much longer. As repeatedly stressed in the previous chapters, the existing fissures in the edifice of European integration are of such fundamental nature that it cannot survive without a thorough renovation. Either we open up space for reimagining of what European integration should look like (and be about), or the project collapses. The following chapter is aimed at doing the former: at trying to think about radically different things that European integration *could* be about. It is about a vision of integration that is more creative, more progressive, more ambitious, and more sensitive to the life that Europe's citizens can actually live.

How to Make Money

The ten proposals that are elaborated in this chapter range from the creation of artworks, an overhaul of the EU's energy infrastructure, and free interrail passes for its citizens. As with all policy ideas, these proposals cost money. To pre-empt any criticism that these ideas are economically unfeasible, I will start this chapter with some ideas on how the EU could generate resources for the implementation of bold and innovative ideas (which, of course, can be radically different from the ones elaborated below). As with the ten proposals that follow, the ideas on how to generate resources do not take account of their legal and political feasibility, nor are all practical implications worked out. Instead, they serve to highlight that another kind of Europe *can* be imagined.

There are at least five relatively obvious sources for the generation of vast resources for the EU. The first sees in the reconfiguration of some of the money that the EU already spends. The Common Agricultural Policy—a fund that supports farmers in securing income, creates incentives for innovative and sustainable farming solutions, and insures farmers against market drops for their products—has a yearly budget of €58.82 billion. To put this into context, the CAP budget is higher than the GDP of *nine* Member States (Luxemburg, Slovenia, Croatia, Bulgaria, Malta, Cyprus, Estonia, Latvia, and Lithuania). Of this sum, €41.74 billion is used to support the income of farmers, who cannot survive on their income generated through sale of produce alone. The objectives of the CAP are, in general terms, to ensure food security for the EU, to protect rural communities from the economic effects of global competition, and to foster innovative solutions for sustainable farming.

While these objectives are certainly valuable, there are perhaps better ways to spend close to €60 billion while securing these objectives. Income support and the protection of rural communities, for example, could also be secured by creating a universal basic income, which protects the income of all citizens and makes urban centres less attractive as places to live. Innovative solutions and sustainable farming would probably best be served by investing heavily in *parts* of the EU where the climate is best suited for particular crops or animal farming (rather than investing in corn or cow farms in every Member State). Investing in urban farms could help reduce waste and make citizens aware of what they eat; while reclaiming farmland for the purpose of wildlife, forests, and national parks will serve wider climate goals.

A second way of sourcing funding is by rethinking defence spending. Currently, EU Member States spend over €200 billion on defence per year, which is likely to rise in the coming years due to North Atlantic Treaty Organization (NATO) commitments and the rising threat of cyber-surveillance and political manipulation. Studies in the Munich Security Studies Report, however, suggest that the EU Member States could save up to €65 billion *a year* by cooperating on military research, the procurement of military equipment, joint operations, and the pooling and sharing of resources.[1] A defence strategy and budget that is centrally coordinated by the EU could not only save an enormous amount of taxpayers' money, but would also allow for a much more effective way of tackling problems that *all* Member States face (e.g., cyber-attacks on its public infrastructure or political meddling by foreign states).

Beyond trying to figure out ways to save money that the Member States already spend, there are also at least three *new* ways of securing vast resources for EU action. The first lies in increasing cooperation between Member States in preventing tax evasion. The past years have seen an investigation in a number of dodgy tax-deals through which some of the richest companies in the world barely pay any taxation at all in Europe. Countries such as the Netherlands, Ireland, and Luxembourg have become sites through which companies such as Apple, Google, Starbucks, and Facebook route their revenues so that they do not have to pay taxes in the other Member States. Just to give an example: Apple, which has a yearly revenue of €245 billion, and is worth more than €1 trillion (just think about that for a second), has for years had a 'sweetheart deal' with Ireland. In return for setting itself up in Ireland, Apple was allowed to 'shield' up to €110 billion of profits from the tax authorities in the EU by sending the money to the Caribbean, paying as little as 0.005% taxation on its European profits. In the meantime, Apple only had to pay 2% in corporate taxation to Ireland. Amazon, in 2016, had a revenue of €21.6 billion in the EU, but only paid €16.5 million in taxation in Luxembourg (where it routes all of its European revenue). This is a taxation rate of 0.076%. It seems that most multinationals (as well as rich entrepreneurs, football players, and musicians) have these deals, which allow them to 'shield' much of their income from taxation.

Part of the problem is that taxation is not regulated on the European level, but instead decided in each capital independently. The result is that rich companies can 'shop around' and locate their headquarters (and sometimes just a letterbox for tax purposes) in the country that offers them the best deal. Not only is it morally indefensible to allow the richest companies to escape taxation that the poorest citizens cannot; it is also a problem that the EU can easily tackle. A European-wide corporate taxation regime, or a new tax on revenue, that demands that *each* company that makes use of the EU's internal market to make money actually returns something to the EU and its citizens, is not just an easy mechanism to prevent tax avoidance, but also a source for unimaginable wealth that can be spent on projects that put the citizen—and not the market—first.

A *compulsory* corporate tax rate of 20% (which is more or less the average that EU Member States currently set), or a revenue tax of 5% on digital products would prevent the Apples and Googles of this world from 'shielding' their income from taxation. These companies, which have amassed unimaginable wealth in the past years, have benefitted from the EU's internal market—and now it is time for a return of the favour. Even if we only look at Apple, Amazon, Google, and Facebook, a 5% revenue tax regime would already generate €4.95 billion per year. If all companies that operate on the internal market are taxed at a minimum of 20%—whether through corporation tax, revenue tax, or another source—this will generate hundreds of billions each year for the EU, its Member States, and its citizens.

A second potential new tax base could be something like a 'personal data' tax. Increasingly, companies are amassing vast wealth by marketing or selling data generated by their users, that is, us citizens. As more and more of our life takes place online, our preferences (when it comes to shoes, flights, sexuality, food, or political affiliation) have become a product. Almost every big company that has emerged over the last decade is primarily involved in harvesting personal information for either the improvement of their services (i.e., making more profit) or for selling that information to third parties. The scandal with Cambridge Analytica and Facebook in 2018 is perhaps the most recent memorable example of that collusion, but, of course, Google's whole business model (which is worth close to a trillion €) is based on ensuring its advertisers that only customers with certain preferences will be targeted.

But the use of personal data for product optimisation occurs equally in airlines, online shops, banks, and hospitals. Harvesting such data allows them to provide their services in a way that is more profitable, or to sell it to companies that find increasingly innovative ways of marketing that information. This is even without taking account of the possible ways in which 'big data' can be marketed. All this is not to pretend that these new tech companies are 'evil' for amassing pools of personal information. For the most part, it is freely supplied by its customers, and the EU's General Data Protection Regulation (GDPR) serves to incorporate some basic safeguards in how personal information is stored and used. Rather, the proposal for a tax on the use of personal data suggests that this information cannot—even if the individual wants to—be given up for *free*. If a company makes money by using the data generated by citizen preferences, they ought to give something *back* to the citizens. A flat-rate tax on companies that use personal data—with the exclusion of public service providers and charities—could be a good starting point in thinking to what extent personal data ought to serve collective purposes rather than profit-making. Even at a low rate, such a taxation scheme would generate billions for the EU.

A third and final new strategy to generate resources for the EU is carbon pricing. This is a proposal that has been mooted repeatedly over the past decades, and most recently by Emmanuel Macron in his speeches on the future of the EU. This includes three elements. First, it includes a tax levied on energy sources that contain carbon, such as coal, natural gas, and petroleum. Second, it comes with a 'carbon border tax', which taxes overseas spending in industries that emit carbon outside of the EU, and, conversely, by non-EU companies that emitted carbon while producing goods that are marketed in the EU. Third, it sets minimum pricing for carbon trading schemes, so that current market-based solutions for carbon reduction price carbon at a level that actually discourages its emission. This form of carbon taxation and carbon pricing serves multiple objectives: it decreases the use of polluting sources of energy; it makes renewable energy more competitive and thereby creates an incentive for innovation; and it offers an additional tax base. An EU-wide rate of around €40 per metric tonne of CO_2 (if we exclude the border tax and the pricing cap, which are more difficult to quantify) would generate a yearly €131 billion in revenue.

Now that we've discussed several possibilities for gathering vast resources on the European level—by taxing carbon emissions, the use of personal data, and the richest companies in the world for their entry to the internal market, and by cooperating on defence and agriculture—let us see how we can put that money to good use.

How to Spend It

The following pages detail ten policy initiatives that radically change what the EU is for. These policies are examples of the type of policies that the EU *could* implement if it were minded to create an EU that is based on trust between its citizens, geared towards the achievement of a specific vision of its future, and committed to engaging its citizens more closely with the direction of the integration process. What these proposals have in common is that they offer ways to construct an EU that is *more European*, and thereby more sensitive to the context within which it operates. These proposals celebrate the diversity of Europe, its accomplishments such as the welfare state, its commitment to a sustainable work-life balance, and its desire to cooperate. To a greater or lesser extent, all proposals build on the more abstract insights that were discussed in the previous chapters.

Each proposal is explained only very briefly, and is costed even more briefly. Whole libraries have been written on some of these proposals. On each, a whole book could be written. The point of the following pages, then, is not to offer an exhaustive theoretical account, guide to practical implementation, legal basis, or economic assessment of the feasibility of each proposal. Rather, the point is to offer a taste of what the EU *could* be about, and how it could help to change our societies for the better.

Proposal 1: Ticket to Ride

Every European receives a free interrail pass for a month when they turn 18 and 65. This allows free travel on all trains in Europe, and is to be used within 4 years.

Let us start with an idea that is so simple and powerful that it has actually been implemented already in part. This is the idea to give all Europeans the chance to travel throughout the continent for free. The original idea to provide all Europeans with a free interrail pass for a month when they turn 18 was developed by two young Germans, Vincent-Immanuel Herr and Martin Speer. Their own introduction to the proposal speaks to the romance of travel and youth. It reads: 'Imagine it is your 18th birthday and you find a personalized letter from the European Commission in your postbox. In it: a voucher to travel Europe. Your life will change.'[2]

Interrail is already very popular. Yearly, 300,000 (mostly young) Europeans use it to travel throughout the continent. No other continent has as many international connections, high-quality trains, and expansive rail network. You can literally travel to the four corners of Europe by public transport. Waking up in Paris, for example, allows a traveller to arrive in Lisbon, Naples, Edinburgh, Krakow, or Bucharest by just making *one* transfer. The EU is already trying to further develop so-called 'corridors' that will facilitate travel throughout Europe. Examples of these 'corridors' are connections between Stockholm and Palermo or that between Sevilla and Budapest. Directing further investment towards the use and expansion of the rail network is—in addition to the immediate objectives of this policy proposal—also clearly of importance for Europe's environmental credentials.

The main attraction of the idea of offering a free interrail pass to all Europeans that turn 18 is, however, not even about investing in transport networks or protecting the environment. Its more immediate objectives are two-fold, and seek to stimulate trust between Europeans.

First of all, travel serves to expose Europeans to other Europeans. If trust is something that emerges from doing the most mundane things imaginable *together*—explaining to a Slovenian ticket controller that you need to make the connection to Trieste; ordering a cheese sandwich at the station of Coimbra; figuring out where to sleep when you arrive late at night in Warsaw—then allowing each European to travel free of charge throughout Europe for a month clearly stimulates this. It allows—in fact necessitates—contact between Europeans in negotiating timetables, new culinary experiences, experiencing nightlife, or finding lodging, as well as exposing the traveller to the differences and similarities between the ways of life of different parts of Europe.

The purpose of this proposal is not to make Europeans *more alike*. As we saw before, the creation of trust does not necessitate homogeneity. It does necessitate, however, being exposed to difference. This proposal would seek to do exactly that. It does so not only by stimulating interaction with fellow Europeans but also by helping the citizen to understand Europe better and helping them to articulate their own account of what Europe means to them. A one-month free travel pass requires each citizen to make a tough decision about where to go (and where not to go). Europe's dazzling diversity becomes very clear once faced with this decision. Are you more curious to visit the cities of great art or the southern beaches? Are you tempted to explore the wilderness and mountains, or the metropoles? Will you see snow or sand for the first time in your life? Are you and your friends interested in visiting the stadiums of all Champions League winners? Do you want to visit the highest dune of Europe in the *Landes* or the northernmost point of Europe in *Nordkapp*? Do you prefer the whisky distilleries in the Scottish Highlands or the wild bears in Transylvania? The diversity of Europe and great variety of possible trips stimulate creativity and curiosity. Like our fathers used to ask each other where they were stationed for their military service, Europeans will now ask each other how they had spent their month interrailing—and all the adventures that they experienced in doing so!

The second objective that underlies this proposal is that it is inclusive. Unsurprisingly, the 300,000 current users of interrail come from the segment of European society that has both time and money to travel. More generally, free movement is used by a very small percentage of Europeans (under 1% permanently resides in another Member State), and research of Eurostat over the course of 2015 shows that over 40% of Europeans do not travel at all, while two-thirds of all trips that do take place are within the citizen's own country.[3] Travelling in Europe, to put it simply, is not for everyone. This proposal would change that. It extends the privilege of travelling through Europe to all Europeans that turn 18—whether they are in school, are about to start university, are unemployed, or are working already. This proposal, then, opens the possibility to discover Europe to a whole new group in society—not just by visiting cities, but by meeting people, tasting foods, and interacting with fellow Europeans. A well-documented network of cheap hostels already exists throughout Europe, and would, presumably, only increase once this initiative is in place. The only headache is in deciding where to go.

I would propose expanding the reach of this project to also include a month's worth of interrail for every European that reaches retirement age (at whatever age that is set in the different Member States). This would—of course—meet the same objectives as described above: it allows retirees to travel cheaply, to discover Europe, to map their own trajectory, and to visit old friends or their favourite holiday destinations. It also, however, celebrates the start of a new phase of their life and signals that life is about more than work. If anything is specific to Europe's 'way of life' when compared to other continents, it must be exactly this: a commitment to a good quality of life *beyond* the workplace. Offering a month of free interrail travel to retirees signals gratitude for their hard work, not only in the workplace, but also in raising families, giving directions to their 18-year-old counterparts in the train stations throughout Europe, and—more generally—playing their part in society.

In the aftermath of Brexit, the leader of one of the parties in the European Parliament took on this interrail project to highlight that the EU is not an elitist project, but reaches out to all Europeans. Starting from the 2018 budget, therefore, the EP has allocated resources to allow—as a pilot—20,000 young Europeans the possibility to travel throughout Europe for a month free of charge. Hopefully to be continued!

Estimated Costs
The average group of recipient per year (18 year olds + 65 year olds) would be around 6.5 million Europeans. The current cost of an Interrail ticket is €493, which would amount to a cost of around €3.2 billion per year. However, Interrail is run by the Eurail Group—which is composed of national rail companies—most of which are in public hands and operate on state licences or subsidies, making it fairly easy to run the project at cost price rather than the commercial rate. A rough estimate would be that this would amount to €100 per traveller—making the budget required for this project €650 million per year. To put that sum in perspective, it could be met simply by making Amazon pay 3% in taxation over their European earnings instead of 0.076%.

Proposal 2: European Basic Income

> Every European receives a guaranteed and unconditional monthly income that allows him or her to have a decent life without having to rely on work.

This second proposal is ambitious. It sees to the establishment of a European-wide basic income, which guarantees sufficient funds for everyone to live an autonomous and dignified life without having to rely on labour. It would offer all Europeans the present of time, revolutionise our societies, and take the sting out of the social consequences of automation.

With the exception of the richest citizens, we all either have money through employment but no time to enjoy it, or lots of time but no money to enjoy it due to unemployment. Only the rich have the luxury of forsaking a job in pursuit of a life that best suits their interest, ambitions, creative drives, or desires. What about the rest of us—who may want to spend time with their children or elder relatives; who may have exceptional creative potential; who would love to volunteer, study, exercise, cook, or help the neighbour instead of commuting, working a dead-end job, worrying about their employment status, and heating up a microwaved dish at the end of another endless day at work? What about my teenage cousins, who when I ask them what they want to become speak full of excitement about drawing, travelling, and football before concluding that they will probably learn to code or work in retail because 'it makes more sense'?

Most of us take it for granted that this is what life today looks like. In fact, we are told that we should be grateful for having a job in the first place—even if it is well below our potential or training—especially in light of the (youth) unemployment rates in Spain, Italy, or Greece, which consistently hover around 50%. Talk about a destruction of creative and intellectual potential! Even for those of us that *do* have work, the relentless competitive pressure, increase in commuting time, and rise in job insecurity have led to skyrocketing numbers of psychological disorders, anxiety, insomnia, and stress.

What we need to do with some urgency is to reinvent life *beyond* the work place. This means that we must prioritise the citizens, their capacities, interests, and desires in life, rather than the way in which they can best serve in the workforce. For the lucky few—and I count myself among those—work is a source of pleasure, socialisation, and stimulation. But for too many, work is the exact opposite. It is mind-numbing, it is hard, and it is boring. What makes today the best moment in time for a radical proposal such as a universal basic income is the advent of a new wave of automation, which, with its machine learning, artificial intelligence, and deep thinking, will replace an estimated 47–80% of current jobs.[4] This revolution has the potential to cause widespread unemployment and destitution, but it also offers the best opportunity we have ever had to rethink the role of work in our societies.

A European basic income would offer each European citizen an unconditional income of around 25% of national GDP. This would amount to £600 per month in the United Kingdom; €530 in Spain; or €274 in Poland. This basic income replaces parts of currently existing social security and social assistance mechanisms (but not those aimed at poverty reduction, or access to education and healthcare). How every citizen spends his or her money is up to them. It is also up to them to decide if they want to work or not.

A basic income would prevent two common problems in the job market of today. It would prevent what is called the employment trap, where citizens are forced to accept underpaid or degrading work out of economic necessity. From now on, unattractive jobs will have to be rethought, automated, or come with better conditions. The negotiating power in the job market, in other words, is changed in favour of the worker. A universal basic income would also prevent the *un*employment trap, where accepting work is unattractive for the poorer segments of society because it means losing access to social assistance and guaranteed income. Finally, it would take the sting out of the decrease of employment possibilities caused by the rise of robotics and machine learning—in fact, it would offer a way for governments to back mass automation without risking bankruptcy, large-scale social unrest, or apocalyptic inequality.

But a basic income does more than restructure the labour market. It has objectives that reach much further. It would probably lead to a geographic reconfiguration of where people live—why be in a busy city if you do not need to be there for work? It would lead to a social and cultural revaluation of work that capitalist society does not currently value: taking care of children and elderly, charity work and volunteering, offering public services or free courses to neighbours. It would lead to an avalanche of creative, innovative, and entrepreneurial ways for individuals of spending their lives, and without doubt alleviate the stress and anxiety that come with capitalism and exclusion from increasingly competitive job market. It is impossible to offer a detailed prognosis on all the changes that will ensue from a model of basic income, but it is clear that it would lead to drastic changes to the way people live, how they raise their children, how they act in their community and interact with their neighbours, and how societies are run. It would change schooling systems, political systems, and what our cities look like. Part of what makes the idea of basic income such a revolutionary and exciting idea, in fact, is that it is impossible to predict what will happen once we liberate ourselves from the need to work. As Arthur C. Clarke, the futurist and visionary author of, among others, *2001: A Space Odyssey*, once said: 'The goal of the future is full unemployment, so we can play'.

Setting up a kind of universal basic income is, obviously, very complex. Hundreds of articles and books have already been written about it—ranging from Thomas More's *Utopia* in 1516 to an important recent work by the Belgian philosophers Philippe van Parijs and Yannick Vanderborght.[5] Critics of the idea of a basic income have attacked its political feasibility, its economic sustainability, and its philosophical premise. And certainly establishing a basic income comes with its challenges. We need to think carefully about its effect on existing welfare regimes, on projects of poverty reduction, its effect on the housing market, tax system, public services, and the educational system.

But while these challenges should not be taken lightly, there is nothing that would make this project impossible if it is what citizens want. The project of establishing a universal basic income starts, to put it starkly, with citizens desiring another kind of future than the one that is currently on offer. Several Member States, including Finland, the Netherlands, and Spain, are currently trialling different systems of basic income on a small scale. While clearly a lot more research needs to done in the structures, funding, and consequences of rolling out a European-wide basic income, the next decades offer, more than ever before, the perfect combination of circumstances for its success: a rapid rise of automation, the need for a new common project that binds (young) Europeans, and a rising awareness of the need to find a better balance between work and play.

Estimated Costs

It is close to impossible to predict the costs of a European-wide basic income, due to the different variations of the basic income scheme that exist, the differences in living costs throughout Europe, the costs of some of the welfare regimes that it will replace, the effect that it will have on the tax revenue through income tax, the probable decrease in healthcare costs, and so on. Suffice to say that several high-profile economists have argued that funding a scheme of universal basic income is feasible through a combination of a slight increase in income tax and saving on other welfare regimes.[6] This is even without considering the potential vast resources in the form of new taxation on data, carbon, and tech revenue, listed at the start of this chapter, which amount to hundreds of billions each year.

Proposal 3: Station Ten

The creation of 10 start-up hubs throughout Europe that group and fund 500 projects and products serving a public purpose.

While Europe has produced companies such as Skype, Spotify, Booking, and ASOS, many still bemoan the lack of a European Silicon Valley. Typically, in these accounts, Silicon Valley is shorthand for a single geographical location that draws the best and brightest people working on cutting-edge projects that have the potential to transform the world. The advantages of such a 'hub' are well documented: the transmission of expertise among start-ups, the fostering of unexpected cooperation, the clustering for investors and graduates, socialisation effects, and feedback opportunities.

European alternatives to the Silicon Valley have emerged over the past decade. London has its 'Silicon roundabout', Berlin has Factory. Lisbon has invested heavily over the past years and now ranks fourth in the world as the best locations to set up a start-up. Paris, with perhaps the most ambitious project of all, has launched a new hub called *Station F*, which, with its 34,000 m², over 100 start-ups, and plans for accommodation for the entrepreneurs, is the biggest in the world. All these cities attempt to do the same thing: to foster innovation, compete to attract the best young minds, introduce the dynamism and internationalism that start-ups bring to the local economy, educational sector, and cultural sector, and to reap the ensuing fiscal and reputational benefits.

This third proposal would stimulate this development, with two big changes. First, the hubs funded by the EU would be decentralised. Second, access would be available for free only for start-ups that deal with projects or products that have a public purpose. At the moment, start-ups are reliant on being able to (eventually) make money. Without this potential, it is difficult to secure funding or attract the best graduates. The start-up economy, in other words, is geared around creating or changing a certain market, around fulfilling a certain specific function. This project would change those basic parameters. The start-ups that receive funding are those that serve a public purpose and contribute to the *common* good.

The European start-up model would be decentralised. Rather than creating *a* European Silicon Valley, it is setting up ten different ones, spread out over Europe. Let's say—for the sake of the argument—that a campus with accommodation for 500 employees and working space for 50 start-ups is set up in Athens, Leipzig, Bucharest, Warsaw, Rotterdam, Helsinki, Paris, Palermo, Lisbon, and Dublin. It might seem that this would defeat the very purpose of creating a start-up hub, as it disperses the expertise, know-how, people, and projects rather than linking them.

However, spreading them out will have two, somewhat contradictory, benefits. First, it makes them more accessible for all Europeans. Every European will have a hub within a few hundred kilometres of their home—which makes participation not just more practical, but also decreases the economic and cultural costs that might otherwise prevent access. Second, it is to be expected that these hubs would organically start to diversify—based on local interests, strengths of local university expertise, local infrastructure, or history. While Athens might draw the best minds to rethink digital democracy, the best minds in the innovation of public spaces might unite in Rotterdam.

The second big change to the usual vision for a European Silicon Valley is that the new campuses, with space for at least 500 start-ups, are exclusively and freely available for start-ups that work, in some way, on *public* projects. These campuses, in other words, serve to foster innovation about the way our societies function. This proposal is certainly not about preventing start-ups from making (a lot of) money. For better or worse, this is still an important driving force in such a competitive environment. Rather, it is a way to signal that, in return for big investments, start-ups can be expected to think about ways in which our collective future can be enriched. And it is a way to signal to the brightest Europeans that their ideas, energy, and intellect can be put to use for the *common* good—and not just in making better ads or lining Zuckerberg's pockets.

Public projects can come in many flavours, and the best ones are without doubt unimaginable at this moment (by me, at least). They might be, first of all, public in the sense that they rethink how our democracies work—such as projects that facilitate digital democracy, weed out fake news stories, allow activist movements, enhance communication between voters or their access to information, rethink the role of minorities or disenfranchised citizens, and so on. Second, the public nature of a project or product might have to do with access to public services. This could include creating freely available MOOCs (massive open online courses that use technology to allow widespread access to university degrees), tech solutions to urban, regional, or even space transport, projects that think about water shortage, new tools for medicine delivery, waste disposal, communication, or labour protection. Projects could also, thirdly, be about creating public events. These could range from setting up free festivals to art projects, from the creation of a website for interrailers to projects that bring history to life through virtual reality. A fourth way in which a project or product could have a public angle is by engaging with how public spaces are used and communities operate. This could mean tech projects that are about community building, about the sharing economy, about rethinking sustainable building materials for houses, or about stimulating urban farming.

These projects are obviously just examples. There are, in fact, endless ways of creating a project or product for the common good. This proposal of creating ten start-up hubs throughout Europe is about creating the incentives for the most creative and ambitious Europeans to work for that common good (rather than optimising ad revenue), about allowing them to engage with the future of Europe, and about creating the infrastructure and financial support structures that bring them together.

Estimated Costs
The creation of these hubs—with big campuses that include working spaces and accommodation—is difficult to cost. Some already exist, and can be drawn into the proposal. Others will need to be created from scratch or require converting existing public spaces—such as old tram depots, shipping yards, or government buildings. Once a hub is operational, the costs are more easily predicted. Station F—the biggest start-up campus in the world with over 100 companies—has a running cost of €8 million per year.[7] The ten hubs in this proposal would be half the size, but would also include funds for accommodation. Start-ups would receive 5-year seed funding of—say—€5 million on average. A rough estimate, then, would put the cost of this proposal (beyond initial infrastructural investment) at around €580 million per year. In other words, this revolutionary and ambitious project could be funded entirely if we'd only make Apple pay 0.53% of taxation on its European earnings.

Proposal 4: A Tale of Two Countries

> Member States are twinned for a year, during which a range of cultural, artistic, culinary, sporting, and educational exchanges take place.

In the last scene of the film *L'auberge espagnole* (translated in English as *Potluck Dinner*), Romain Duris, who plays the main protagonist, looks back on his year spent in Barcelona on Erasmus exchange. After surveying the cheerful chaos that was his flatshare—which included Belgian, Danish, Spanish, Italian, English, and German friends—and thinking about the changes he personally had gone through during the year, he concludes: '*je suis comme l'Europe; je suis un vrai bordel*'. This sentence doesn't translate very nicely in English, but perhaps comes closest to: '*I'm like Europe; I'm a right mess*'.

What he means by this is that he understands himself to be a cheerful, chaotic, and illogical combination of different parts. He is at once conformist and revolutionary; shy and exuberant; and mean yet kind. He is—like Europe—made up out of irreconcilable, surprising, and dysfunctional parts that somehow make an interesting whole. This fourth proposal seeks to make the 'mess' that is Europe visible to all. It would bring to all Europeans—not just those that go on Erasmus or can travel—a taste of the dazzling diversity of Europe, and the feelings of similarity, disorientation, and shock that come with it.

Every three years, Member States are twinned for the duration of one year. Let's say that for the duration of 2020, for example, Sweden and Portugal are twinned, as are Greece and Poland. The EU would fund a wide variety of exchanges between these countries, so that everyone—regardless of their interest in photography, wine, football, bird-spotting, history, food, hiking, children's songs, or computer games—can participate.

This could take place in thousands of different ways: Portugal and Sweden could set up a weekend in which they compete in football and tennis, but also in sports that are popular in only one of both countries—such as bandy (look it up!), ice hockey, or canoeing. Swedish children in primary school could learn a song in Portuguese to amuse their parents with. High school kids from Coimbra could spend a week on exchange in

Sundsvall—and perhaps see snow for the first time in their lives, taste fermented herring and cinnamon buns, and understand what a sauna is about. The MAAT (Museum of Art, Architecture, and Technology) museum in Lisbon and the Moderna Museet in Stockholm could exchange parts of their collection so that more Europeans can appreciate it. In summer, festivals would introduce Portuguese audiences to the work of Ingrid Bergman and Lykke Li, and Swedish audiences to *Fado*, port wine, and *pasteis de nata*.

The point of all these different types of exchanges is *not* to make Europeans more alike. The point is, in fact, the exact opposite: to make Europeans understand that they are different. Whether this is done by watching TV-series such as *The Bridge*, documentaries about the Carnation Revolution, or tasting each other's food; it will be clear to all participants that Sweden and Portugal are very different places, with a different mentality. Swedes would learn about the decriminalisation of hard drugs in Portugal. The Portuguese would learn that 16% of Swedes believe in ghosts. Swedes would be exposed to the question of how to deal with the legacy of colonialism, while Portuguese might marvel at the midsummer celebrations and how important light and sun are for other cultures. The Swedes would struggle to grasp the untranslatable concept of *saudade* as much as the Portuguese would struggle with the equally untranslatable *fika*. These exchanges are meant to induce bewilderment, amusement, jealousy, shock, and pleasure.

As we saw before, trust between citizens, and thereby their willingness to cooperate, is not necessarily premised on being alike. It is premised on understanding that even though you might be different, these differences are contingent. This is a complicated way of saying that things *can* be done differently. The food, the setting, and the timing of breakfast might be unrecognisable between Porto and Malmö, but it serves the same function. The exploits of the Vikings and Vasco da Gama have very little in common, but have a similar mythical status in the self-understanding of the Swedes and Portuguese. The work of Fernando Pessoa and ABBA is miles apart, yet both remain important cultural reference points in their own country.

Both empirical and theoretical work suggests that being exposed to these kinds of differences is good for two reasons. The first reason is that being exposed to other ways of doing things demystifies difference. It shows that what makes a Portuguese national a Portuguese national is just a different historical and geographical context in which similar choices (what to have for breakfast, what music to listen to, which political questions are salient) have been made. It also, reflexively, shows that what makes a Swedish national a Swedish national is equally contingent, that is, dependent on pretty random geographical, historical, or political circumstances. Being exposed to all this, then, makes people more understanding of difference *and* of themselves, without trying to overcome these differences.

The second way in which being exposed to the 'mess' that is Europe is helpful in the construction of trust between its citizens is because, simply put, it makes them resent each other less. Getting to know another culture, and another 'way of doing things', especially in a ritualised context such as country-twinning, does not necessarily lead to citizens liking the other country better. A Portuguese school kid who spent a week in Sundsvall might be more convinced than ever before that *bacalhau* is better than fermented herring and that Zlatan Ibrahimović was half the football player that Cristiano Ronaldo was. What it does lead to, however, is that the Portuguese kid will be more positively predisposed towards Sweden, probably for the rest of his life. In the words of Richard Sennett, the sociologist whose work we looked at before: 'ritualised moments which celebrate the differences between members of a community, which affirm the distinctive value of each person, can diminish the acid of invidious comparison and promote cooperation'.[8] What this means, in simple terms, is that being exposed to difference is useful for cooperation because understanding someone makes citizens less suspicious of that person and his intents. Familiarity, as we know by now, breeds trust.

Estimated Costs

The projects that the EU currently undertakes that serve somewhat similar goals—such as Creative Europe, which funds the production and dissemination of films, books, and festivals throughout Europe—have a budget of €1.4 billion (which is 0.15% of the EU's budget). It is difficult to estimate exactly how much this proposal of twinning countries might cost. But let's presume that each 'twinning' receives €200 million to organise projects—whether educational exchanges, culinary festivals, or the production of documentaries—in which they introduce each other. Even such a generous sum, available once every three years, would add just €933 million to the EU's expenditure per year (0.1% of the EU's current budget—even discounting the possible source of revenue listed at the start of this chapter).

Proposal 5: The Green Deal

Large-scale investment in wind turbines and solar parks, as well as the infrastructure to connect the whole EU to the same grid, so that 100% of the EU's electricity consumption comes from sustainable and renewable sources.

This fifth proposal is so wildly ambitious that, like the proposal for a European basic income, it has the potential to change the very purpose and nature of the EU. It would see a large-scale public investment, unseen since the Marshall Plan, to set up a state-of-the-art electricity grid throughout the EU that operates exclusively on renewable energy. This would meet several objectives at once: it would help combat climate change; it would offer a new purpose for the EU that all coming generations can rally around; it would create jobs and investment in the some parts of the EU that are the very poorest; and it would create a wealth of innovation, research, and industries that can be sold and exported around the world.

The aspiration to achieve political ends by large-scale public works is not new, of course. Roosevelt's New Deal, with which he reconfigured the economic and political infrastructure of the United States in the 1930s, is perhaps the best example. But around that same time, another project—much closer to the one discussed here—was doing the rounds of Europe. The project was named *Atlantropa* and was the brainchild of the German architect Herman Sörgel. He proposed to build a hydroelectric dam across the Strait of Gibraltar, effectively sealing off the Mediterranean, which would decrease its water level up to 200 metres. This would, in his view, serve a range of objectives: it would be a source of unlimited electricity; it would create more land within the Mediterranean basin to counter the emerging tensions of the lack of space and agricultural land; it would link Europe to African hinterlands that were full of natural resources; and it would unite the European countries in support of this large-scale project.

Sörgel's vision was that this project would take up so much manpower and money from the participating countries that they would be unable to start a new war. Once the new dam was active, moreover, an independent commission would oversee the new energy supply and would be able to cut off the supply to any country that threatened the peace in Europe. A second dam, linking Sicily to Tunisia, would generate even more electricity, as well as—bizarrely—allowing a weekly train service between Berlin and Cape Town. Sörgel championed this idea until his death, which was never considered feasible due to its large scale—in fact, there were even doubts whether enough concrete existed in the world in the 1940s to build the dam. Today, his project reeks of colonialism, and the impact on the ecology and topography of the Mediterranean basin seems particularly devastating.

The proposal here would be a variation on Sörgel's plan—in keeping with his aspirations rather than with his execution. It would start with the same logic: an unlimited energy supply, combined with an electricity grid that connects the four corners of Europe would not only be an ecological marvel, but also serve as a new focal point for European cooperation, and, once active, as the perfect inhibitor for antagonism between interdependent countries.

Clearly, this proposal is based on a long-term plan. It requires research in technological innovations to create more efficient turbines and solar panels; better and bigger batteries to store excess energy; and a state-of-the-art electricity grid that links the sources of electricity to the households of Turku, Rennes, and Zagreb. The new infrastructure—vast parks full of wind turbines and massive solar farms—would be concentrated where they are most effective. Today, each Member State plans its own turbines and solar farms, irrespective of the relative efficiency. Partially, this is for reasons of energy security. Partially, it is because the grid that might transport electricity from one Member State to the next is not harmonised and able to transport the quantities of electricity required across borders. This proposal would change that. Wind turbines could be clustered in the eastern provinces of Romania, in the Spanish mountains, off the Irish coast, in the North Sea, and in the Baltic Sea. Large-scale solar farms would be created where solar potential is the highest: in the Algarve, Andalucía, Extremadura, Castilla-La Mancha, Malta, Sardinia, Sicily, Puglia, and across the Peloponnesus and the Greek islands.

The ecological benefits of this project are evident. If 100% of the electricity used in Europe comes from renewable sources (as it already does on the Greek island of Tilos), it would lead to a decrease in hundreds of giga-tonnes of carbon dioxide. The supply of electricity, moreover, would not just be sustainable but also unlimited, and would be so cheap and ubiquitous that it forces whole industries to switch to electricity as their energy source (such as, e.g., cars). Economically, it would divert investment towards some of the poorest regions of the EU, across its periphery, and give a much-needed economic boost to the local economy. The expertise and technology created by this project, moreover, could be shared or sold across the world. Danish manufacturers alone, for example, have a revenue of €3 billion just from selling its state-of-the-art wind turbines. This is even without accounting for the possibility to sell the surplus electricity to third states. The European Environmental Agency, just to give a sense of the potential of wind energy, has calculated that enough wind can be harvested on a yearly basis to serve Europe's energy needs 20 times over![9] Selling this surplus energy would easily fund all the rest that the EU does.

But while all these benefits are relatively straightforward, the political potential of this proposal is at least as important. As we have seen, European integration is in urgent need of a common purpose that links all its citizens. Renewable energy is one of the few things, in fact, that *already* does this. Over 80% of Europeans are supportive when it comes to renewable and sustainable sources of electricity.[10] A project that links all regions of Europe together in a large-scale progressive project would not only offer a new focal point for integration (i.e., a new *reason* to cooperate), but also, importantly, offer a narrative of sustainability that will convince the younger generations that the integration project is still relevant. Once a new electricity grid that operates exclusively on renewable energy is active, moreover, it will only further strengthen the cooperation between Member States. As we saw earlier, after all, shared intentionality and interdependence are powerful sources of trust. When you depend on your neighbour for switching the light on or charging your phone, to put it as bluntly as possible, you don't start a fight with him.

Estimated Costs

All large-scale public works projects are difficult to cost, and this one especially. Technological advances continuously increase the efficiency of generators and batteries, and push down the costs of turbines and solar farms. A new European super-grid is already in place in roughly 20% of Europe. Despite this, it is clear that the costs of this project can only be expressed in the trillions of Euros. This proposal would need three types of investment: investment in large numbers of wind turbines and solar farms; investment in battery capacity; and investment in the grid infrastructure that allows transmission across the EU.

A rough estimate suggests that the distribution network needs to be expanded by around 65,000 kilometres, which, on current prices, comes down to €196 billion. If we take the EU's current electricity consumption, and go for an energy mix of 33% solar, 33% onshore wind, and 33% offshore wind, this would require significant expansion in solar farms and turbines. If we—for the sake of calculation—locate these in Southern Italy, Spain, and the United Kingdom, respectively, and use the current capacity factor, this would entail an investment of €242 billion in solar farms, €629 billion in onshore wind turbines, and €1.4 trillion in offshore wind turbines. Finally, the cost for a four-hour storage capacity that could store excess electricity of this quantity would be €149 billion. The total costs for 100% renewable electricity in the EU would come to €2.31 trillion.[11]

How such a sum could be generated is the obvious next question. Beyond government investment and the sources of funding discussed at the beginning of this chapter, a few other options exist. As Project Drawdown's own projections suggest, for example, a move towards renewables offers a significant return on investment: 'an increase in onshore wind from 3% to 4% of world electricity use to 21.6% by 2050 could reduce emissions by 84.6 gigatonnes of carbon dioxide. At a cost of $1.23 trillion, wind turbines can deliver net savings of $7.4 trillion over three decades of operation. These are conservative estimates, however. Costs are falling annually and new technological improvements are already being installed, increasing capacity to generate more electricity at the same or lower cost.'[12] The EU could also issue some sort of 'climate bond' that are secured against the revenues generated by the unlimited amount of electricity generated. Likewise, if the projections of the European Environmental Agency are correct, the potential for wind energy alone is sufficient to meet Europe's energy needs 20 times over. Just imagine the revenue that could be generated if that surplus energy would be sold. It would—without exaggeration—comfortably fund the nine other proposals in this list.

Proposal 6: Concrete Europe

> Every five years, a similar artwork or monument is offered to every Member State. It is up to the Member State to decide what to do with it.

The EU is all around us. Its rules regulate the labelling of the bottle of water on your table, the composition of your make-up, safety of the baby-carrier that you use, and the privacy settings on your social media account. And yet, the EU is all but invisible. The only place in daily life where one might discern a small European flag is when passing a new road or bridge that has been built with EU funding, or at the start of a movie that has been co-funded by the Creative Europe project. Beyond these examples, the EU operates in the shadows. This is a problem: it is difficult to engage with Europe when you are not confronted with it.

The nation state, on the other hand, has physical and symbolic manifestations everywhere: from the ambulance that passes you in the street to the colour of the licence plates, from the stamps that you use to the mailman or the bus driver. These symbols matter: by giving a more immediate presence to the state, it allows people to engage with it.

Some of the most powerful symbols of the state are its public spaces. We take it for granted that when France wins the World Cup, we see millions of people on the *Avenue des Champs-Élysées*. The images of the tearing down of the Berlin wall in 1989 are some of the most powerful of the last century. When Greek citizens protested against the austerity drive, they gathered in Syntagma Square, in front of their national parliament. The 2011 riots in London started with the burning down of state symbols: police cars and buses. These symbols of state power are useful because they offer a focus, or a site, through which to engage with the state: whether to celebrate its glory, tear down its past, or protest some of its actions.

The best recent example of how physical manifestations of the state become a site for public engagement is the controversy around the *Valle de los Caídos* in Spain. This site—which holds an enormous monument (partially built into a rockface) as well as a Catholic basilica—was built under instructions of Franco to commemorate those who died during the Spanish Civil War. It has been a site of controversy for decades now, partially because Franco himself is buried there, and partially because political prisoners had been forced to help construct it. When, in the early 2000s, the socialist government led by Zapatero decided to rid the country of Francoist symbols, they faced a problem: what to do with this massive monument—perhaps the most conspicuous public manifestation of Franco?

The discussion that followed, and is going on today, is the perfect example of the importance of public symbolism. The camps are split between supporters and opponents of the monument, and it is not difficult to read wider claims about Spain's future in the different arguments. Some suggest that Franco's remains ought to be removed, and the site transformed into a place for a commemoration of the deaths during the Spanish Civil War and the Francoist regime. Others want it untouched—either out of sympathy with Franco or to prevent a volatile public discussion on Spain's past. Others object to what the site says about the close relationship between the Catholic church and the Spanish state. Some simply want to tear it down altogether. This is a perfect example of how a physical manifestation of the state can serve as a proxy for public engagement with the past and future of that state.

This sixth proposal would seek to offer such proxies. Every five years, each Member State receives a large monument or artwork funded by the EU. These twenty-seven monuments are similar to each other. The artist could be a world-famous architect or sculptor, or a young graduate from art school. The artist is, obviously, free to make allusions to European integration or not. It could, for example, be a monument made out of material that erodes, showing the fragility of integration; or a work in the style of Tito's Second World War monuments, exuding a utopian vision of the future; or simply a modernist slab of concrete. It could be whimsical, dystopian, or anything in between.

The Member States can decide where they want the monument to be built: some might elect to put it in a town's square, others in the middle of the forest. Some Member States may hold a competition between its cities to host the monument, while others will put it right outside the main airport, in the sea, or in an industrial suburb somewhere. Some might even destroy it. Some citizens might detest the EU but quite like the monument, while others, in favour of the EU, may think that the monument is hideous and a waste of money. Some monuments will be vandalised and covered in graffiti. Some might become places where local kids meet for their first cigarette, others become tourist destinations, while others will fall in disrepair after its first 12 years. Some Europeans might be curious to see where other Member States have placed their monuments. Locals—throughout Europe—will have a very different relationship with the monument that was suddenly placed in their town, beach, or forest.

The point of this proposal is quite simple: it doesn't matter what the monument looks like, or whether the monument is heavily criticised, placed in the middle of nowhere, or covered in graffiti. Its purpose is not to be a pristine and untouched monument. Rather, its purpose is to become a site and a symbol for engagement with what Europe is and what Europe should be. This can be very immediate: Member States will need to decide where to put it (and with this decision comes, again, a lot of symbolic interaction with the idea of Europe), how to act if it is vandalised, and whether to allow protest marches in favour or against European integration to use it as a rallying point. The more diffuse way in which these monuments will become important for the citizens' capacity to engage with Europe is that it makes European integration part of the fabric of society. These visual markers matter greatly in the citizen's awareness of Europe as something that is public, tangible, and accessible. It makes, in a sense, Europe much more concrete than a newly built road ever can.

Estimated Costs

If we take as an example one of the bigger monuments built in recent years, we should be able to predict the cost of this project. The Angel of the North, built in Gateshead (in Northern England), is a steel statue of an angel with outstretched wings, which is 54 metres across and 20 metres high. This giant sculpture cost about €900,000 to build. If we calculate a budget of €1 million for the material, artist fee, and transport per monument, we are being generous. That would mean a total cost of €27 million, or €5.4 million per year. This is about the amount that the European Parliament yearly spends on furniture and furniture maintenance.

Proposal 7: What's for Lunch?

Free school lunches for all Europeans

What links the fight against obesity and the climate challenge? What has the potential to improve the equality and trust between children, and educates them to live a healthy and sustainable life? The answer is, perhaps surprisingly, school lunches.

This proposal would offer free school lunches for all Europeans. In several European countries, these lunches already exist: in some they are semi-compulsory, in others an alternative to bringing to school lunch boxes. In some countries the nutritious value of school lunches equals that of a fastfood 'restaurant', while other countries or regions offer a healthy and balanced choice. Some countries do not have a system for school lunches in place at all. In the Netherlands, for example, it is not uncommon for high school kids to have 15 minutes between classes to eat their bread—in the classroom.

In this proposal, the EU would fund healthy school lunches for all school kids. These lunches would be nutritious and contain close to the daily prescribed amounts of fruit, vegetables, and fibre. Schools could have access to extra funding for setting up their own vegetable patch, urban garden, or orchard; as well as for offering cooking classes on their curriculum. Every day, two dishes are available (one option being vegetarian), and the menu changes regularly to account for different seasons, flavours, and tastes. The menu would reflect the food that grows in the region, the season, as well as the nutritional needs of the children. Kids would go home at the end of the day with their nutritional demands met.

This proposal attempts to tackle a number of issues at once: fighting childhood obesity, improving equality among kids, raising awareness of the footprint of food and its local alternatives, educating children in cooking and taking care of their nutritional needs, and reducing healthcare expenses. Let us take these one by one.

According to the Obesity World Atlas, up to 30% of kids in Europe are overweight. The levels of sugar, salt, and fat consumed by the majority of kids are well above the norm; and, as Jaap Seindell, a Dutch professor in nutrition and health, puts it: '99 percent of kids don't eat enough vegetables, and 90% consumes too little fruit, fish and fiber'.[13] Parents increasingly struggle to offer a nutritious and healthy diet to their children: between coming home from work late, the rising price of fresh food, and the ease of microwavable alternatives, children are eating less nutritious meals every year. Ensuring that all kids have at least one nutritious meal per day in school would go a long way to tackle these problems.

There is ample research that suggests that shared school lunches promote trust between children, and increase their cognitive abilities in school. Neither is particularly surprising. Eating identical food reduces what are called 'invidious comparisons'. Such comparisons—which produce positive feedback for those with the 'coolest' lunch, clothes, or bikes, and negative peer feedback for those who do not—are like kryptonite for trust. They indicate inequality and are the source of the jealousy and/or arrogance that inhibits cooperation. Eating the same meal as your peers, in the same setting, all together, does the exact opposite: it is a great leveller, allowing children to see their classmates as peers and possible sources of cooperation.

That healthy food improves the cognitive abilities of children is clear, as well. Just like athletes eat certain meals in order to improve their performances, so too school children must eat nutritious meals in order to stimulate their minds that are busy learning tools, insights, and both cognitive and social abilities that will serve them for the rest of their lives. A trial that took place in the United Kingdom between 2009 and 2011, where all school kids were offered free lunches in Durham, Newham, Wolverhampton, and Islington, offered evidence for this: after two years, the kids who had access to nutritious lunches in school were on average two months ahead of their peers on academic performance.[14]

A more indirect objective of this proposal is to teach kids about sustainable and healthy food choices. A 2012 survey in the United Kingdom found that 98% of parents thought cooking should be on the school curriculum. All kids could, for example, be presumed to be able to cook a number of healthy meals by the time they graduate. Schools could have their own vegetable patch or roof garden and create projects around certain foods, seasons, or regions. Awareness of how food is grown, which food is indigenous, and which food is nutritious would be part of the learning process.

The substance of the school meals would, of course, differ from school to school, and from region to region. The Sweetgreen charity has undertaken a photo project that offers a good view of the current variety of school lunches, ranging from *gazpacho* and rice with *gambas* (Spain) or roast beef with beans, apples, and cheese (France) to the Greek salad, pomegranate seeds with yoghurt (Greece), and rice or beetroot, fish stew, and pancake (Finland). The EU's task would clearly not be to set the menu for all European school kids. It can, however, disseminate easy and nutritious recipes that take account of seasonal vegetables and local customs, and train school (or town) cooks to be as creative and innovative as they can be: as long as the result is a balanced and nutritious diet.

Estimated Costs
Research in the United Kingdom and the Netherlands, where school meals are not universal, and where their introduction has been debated, has put the cost of a nutritious meal at around €2 per child per day. Given that these countries are some of the more expensive in the EU, a calculation on the basis of €2 per child per day should give us ample space for extra funding for infrastructure changes in schools, the building of vegetable patches, roof gardens, or cooking classrooms. Eurostat numbers suggest that between primary school (28,746,700 children), lower secondary school (20,594,500), and upper secondary school (21,815,900), this proposal would cover around 71 million children.

Serving all these kids a healthy meal for every day that school is in session would cost €28.4 billion per year. This gigantic sum (even though it's only a third of the projected *yearly* savings that could be made by European cooperation on military equipment) comes with a number of caveats. First of all, a large part of this sum is already on the books in the budget of the Member States that provide for free school lunches. In that sense, it is largely the case of shifting the budget to the EU level. Secondly, a contribution of €1 per day by parents (with a maximum of €200 per year) would half the costs to €14.2 billion. Third, the EU already spends €250 million on refunding schools for their (local) purchase of fruit, vegetables, and milk. Finally, the costs of providing free and nutritious school meals are likely to be largely outweighed by future savings in healthcare costs (in particular in relation to diabetes and coronary diseases).

Proposal 8: Our House, in the Middle of the Street

> Every two years, the EU funds a project for every million inhabitants. It is up to the citizens to decide what this project should be about—as long as it is freely accessible to all.

One of the most common criticisms of the EU and, more generally, modern society is that citizens no longer engage. This criticism comes in many flavours. Citizens do not vote for the elections anymore; they feel the EU is too 'remote' from their daily needs and preoccupations. At the same time, there is a more widespread retreat from the community in which one lives. Some blame gentrification, others centralisation of decision-making, and others yet blame capitalism and its relentless competitive drive. What connects all these criticisms is a feeling of loss of control over what one's life looks like. Whether it is because of the distance of politics, or the impossibility to contest the basic shapes of capitalist society, people are increasingly numbed. The French sociologist Emile Durkheim came up with a wonderful word for this state of mind: *anomie*. Anomie describes a sort of mismatch between how individuals see themselves and the collective vision of society that is imposed on them. In much simpler words, it means a fragmentation of society into individuals that no longer communicate in a meaningful way, or no longer work together to create a common vision of society.

This eighth proposal—in a very modest way—seeks to counter this trend. It offers a way in which communities can reassemble, and individual citizens can build up the trust networks and create collective projects that describe *common* visions of society. The idea is that the every two years, the EU funds—for every million inhabitants—a public project. This can be whatever citizens want it to be, as long as it is freely accessible for all. Communities are allowed to come up with whatever idea they want, which is presented to fellow citizens and ultimately voted on electronically. If people in Andalucía think their communities could use free water taps throughout the region, they can come together and campaign for it. If Berliners would like a free open-air cinema, or the inhabitants of Crete a new orphanage, they could get it. What will come out of these projects will likely surprise us all. It is impressive what people can do with a little bit of passion, creativity, and financial support.

But the outcomes of these projects are, of course, not their point. While it is important that local communities can improve their lives through the establishment of public projects, what is even more important is the process through which these projects emerge.

The point of the proposal, in simple terms, is that it makes people cooperate. The carrot of being able to spend €2 million on a public project is such that it creates an incentive for local people to get together with like-minded neighbours, think through a proposal, and campaign to win the support of the wider community. It leads to more interaction within communities, more discussion about what the community is about, and what it lacks. It forces people to think about their collective future, and to weigh against each other alternative visions of that future. It will no doubt lead to disagreement between different proposals, and it will create the need for communities to bridge such disagreement. Some projects will fail, while others will be so successful that neighbouring regions may want to copy them. All winning proposals could be showcased on an online platform that is easily accessible for all other Europeans. In a sense, this proposal offers a large-scale experiment in community building: what Sicilians have come up with in 2024 might bring together the citizens in Eastern Poland for a project in 2026.

All these aspects—more citizen engagement, more communication among citizens, more discussion about a collective future, more need to negotiate disagreement, and more opportunities to learn from each other—are important in reassembling communities in a time where society is becoming increasingly complex and diverse. The explicitly *public* nature of the proposal, moreover, forces this process to be about visions of a common future, in which all members play a role.

Stimulating discussions about community life and public projects on the local level is, of course, also important for the EU's stability. As we discussed in this book, for the EU to transition into something that articulates new *collective* aspirations, and into something that is committed to democratic participation and engagement, one thing above all is crucial: trust networks. Trust networks have a magical property: they emerge organically when a group of like-minded people passionately defend a certain vision of life, community, or society. As soon as this vision is internalised within a system of rule, moreover, trust networks help to stabilise that system. The logic is simple: one the one hand, it makes the EU responsive to what citizens want. On the other hand, it makes citizens want to engage with the EU because it allows them to achieve their objectives. This proposal is, from that perspective, about creating an incentive for citizens, and their like-minded fellow Europeans, to publically articulate the kind of society that they want to live in.

Estimated Costs

For once, a proposal makes for an easy calculation. The EU's current population is 512 million. Taking account of the odd boundary problem (it makes little sense to link Malta and Cyprus in the same project), let's set the number of projects at 530. This would mean a budget of €530 million per year, or, to put this in perspective, 0.92% of the current yearly budget available for the EU's Common Agricultural Policy.

Proposal 9: Eurovision

> A Europe-wide public TV channel and streaming service that broadcasts both regional and international news and makes available to all Europeans programmes produced by national public broadcasters.

This proposal sees to the establishment of a new public TV network and streaming service. The channel would make its own content, collect the best programmes currently produced by national public broadcasters, and make them available throughout Europe. It would offer both Europe-wide and local news, and broadcast big Europe-wide events. The purpose of this new channel is to celebrate what binds Europeans as well as what distinguishes them.

More precisely, this proposal has three objectives. The first is to introduce to all Europeans the wealth of diversity that is Europe. It is one thing to highlight that diversity by making travel more affordable, or by arranging cultural exchanges. It is another thing altogether if we bring this diversity—literally—home: by making it available on demand with a touch of a button while sitting on the couch of your living room. The wealth of diversity of Europe's game-shows, thrillers, but also festivals, geographies, cities, languages, art, cuisine, or music should be for all to see. Learning to understand differences, after all, is important in the construction of trust between citizens, and solidifies their willingness to cooperate with each other.

The second objective of this proposal is to show Europeans what *binds* them. A Danish TV-series about politics might be very helpful in shedding light on the current situation in Bulgarian politics, as much as a Spanish movie might turn out to be a hit in Ireland. Events such as Eurovision or the final of the UEFA Champions League are watched by hundreds of millions of Europeans spread out over the whole continent. These are important markers of popular culture that bind Europeans and that make them understand that—regardless of how different they might be—they also share certain predispositions, views on life, or a preference for certain football players.

The third objective of this proposal is that it provides a place for the dissemination of information and news throughout Europe. As we saw in our discussion on the future of Europe's politics, access to the same information and discussions is indispensible for a vibrant democracy. Citizens must be able to hear the German chancellor say what she makes of the future of Europe, whether it is in Stuttgart, or in Vilnius and Thessaloniki. The making of a European public sphere, in which citizens talk to each other and engage with the European project, requires a continent-wide dissemination of similar information, contrasting political views and freely accessible critical engagement with the choices that politicians make.

What would such a TV network and streaming service look like? How would it be accessible to all Europeans, despite their differences in languages, styles, and interests? Let's take the news, for example. Will it be read in English and focus on news from around the continent? Would that appeal to the Greek or Czech citizen? No, of course not. But technologically it is not particularly difficult to have simultaneous newscasts that are presented in 22 different languages, by 22 different presenters, and that focus the first 15 minutes on the same, Europe-wide, news items, and spend the last 15 minutes on regional news. Technology would allow the Portuguese expat in Berlin to see this newscast in Portuguese with focus on German news, or in German with a focus on Portuguese news. The technology required for instantaneous subtitling is improving quickly—and, in any event, is something that the EU may want to invest in. ARTE, the Franco-German TV channel, for example, also offers its programmes online with English, Polish, and Spanish subtitles. All TV programmes or movies will be available on demand—in its original language with subtitles available for all European languages (and beyond).

But let's leave the theory behind for now—how a public TV network might stabilise relationships of trust and foster public engagement throughout Europe—and imagine what this streaming service and TV channel might broadcast.

The first category of entertainment that will be available for all Europeans are those documentaries, series, or films that have *already* been funded by use of public money. This includes those programmes made by national public broadcasters, but also movies that are (co-)financed by the EU's Creative Europe project. The wealth of shows and movies that this first category includes is mind-boggling. It includes award-winning documentaries such as *Planet Earth*, wildly popular series such as *Borgen*, *The Bridge*, *Commissario Montalbano*, or *Tatort*. Access to funding under the EU's Creative Europe programme for movies could come with an obligation to make any movie available for 12 months on the new platform.

Over the past years alone, this includes the critically acclaimed and commercially successful *La Grande Bellezza*, *Intouchables*, *The Square*, *Trainspotting*, *The Lobster*, *La Vita è Bella*, *The King's Speech*, *Good Bye, Lenin!*, *Festen*, *Amelie Poulain*, *Slumdog Millionaire*, *Call Me by Your Name*, or *Volver*. For the 2018 Oscars, seven nominees have been cofinanced by the EU. All these movies will become available for free for all Europeans—at home, on their mobile, or while travelling, and subtitled in a language of choice.

A second category of shows that will become available is content produced by the new network itself. This can relate to news shows, TV-shows, series, or movies. This new channel would receive a budget for the production of original content shows, not unlike Netflix, and will be able to connect some of the most exciting young producers, actors, and directors in Europe. It would also produce transnational programmes, such as game-shows in which competitors from different regions in Europe compete—in cooking, dancing, on *Fort Boyard*, or in a reboot of the *Jeux sans Frontières*. It could have shows dedicated to introducing European festivals (ranging from *La Tomatina* to *Midsummer*, and from *Palio* and the Dutch *Koningsdag* to *Oktoberfest* and harvest festivals in the Czech Republic). There could be travel shows that showcase the beauty, funkiness, and peculiarities of each European region. The best music festivals from across Europe—from *Roskilde* to *Primavera Sound*—could be broadcast, and every Sunday from 8 to 10 pm we could see the highlights of the football matches in all of Europe's leagues. The channel could show events that draw crowds from across the continent, such as Eurovision, the European football championships, or the Olympics; it could invest in VR so that all Europeans can feel what it's like to watch the band *Phoenix* in Marseille, dive off the Croatian coast, or see the *aurora borealis*.

The third category of programmes that would be available is more serious and seeks to offer a public face to the EU's functioning. The purpose of those programmes is to offer a place for information, contestation, and accountability of the political choices that the EU makes. The channel would offer space for news, investigative journalism, political commentary and satire, talk-shows, and documentaries about the EU and its functioning. It is indispensible for the EU's democratic legitimacy that controversy about its choices is mediatised, that its politicians are held accountable in front of an audience of 500 million Europeans, and that similar themes and discussions can be heard throughout the EU.

In addition to the creation of this new European *public* channel, the rules on geo-blocking should be reconsidered, so that private TV channels or streaming services can also provide the same service throughout Europe.

Estimated Costs

Most of the documentaries, series, and movies that would appear on this new public channel have already been funded through other public funds, and could be made available for free. The real costs for the new channel would be those relating to news and investigative journalism; to translation and subtitling; and to the production of a number of transnational shows or original content. A yearly budget of €1 billion for reporting, content production, and translating services would make for a service that Europeans would be proud to use (for free!). This sum is roughly the budget for public TV in the Netherlands, or for original content production in Europe of Netflix. It would be 0.6% of the EU's yearly budget, or 1.54% of the yearly savings that could be made if Member States were to purchase military equipment jointly.

Proposal 10: A Day for the Future

A new public holiday for all Europeans, in which not the past but the future is celebrated.

Almost all public holidays celebrate or commemorate the past. Their very point is, in fact, to emphasise what people have in common, what binds them: a certain religion, the shared horrors or glory of war, the royal house, or the date of a specific historical event. Some public holidays are similar across the Member States—such as Christmas and Easter—and celebrate certain religious beliefs. Others are purely national, such as the Dutch *Koningsdag* or *Quatorze Juillet*. Yet others, such as the *Palio* in Siena, or the *Fêtes de Bayonne,* celebrate local history and culture. The symbolic importance of public holidays should not be underestimated. As we saw before, what holds nation states together—what binds the Sicilian factory worker with the shepherd in Alto Adige—is a narrative of shared history. National holidays, just as a national flag, the national anthem, or a royal house, are symbols of such a shared history. They offer moments of the year that stand out of the daily grind of working and commuting, and instead are full of rituals that involve family, friends, and full of celebrations that invoke community—whether through attending the Midnight Mass, walking around Amsterdam dressed up in orange, drinking in Bayonne dressed up in red-white, or by respecting a minute of silence in memory of the victims of war.

When, in the failed Constitutional Treaty in the early 2000s, negotiators decided to introduce Europe Day (on 9th May) as a new holiday, mass ridicule ensued. While it meant to commemorate the signing of the Schumann Declaration, which was at the basis of the integration project, many citizens felt it was an artificial move to somehow create a European identity from scratch. The same criticism was levied at the other symbols that the Constitutional Treaty laid down officially, such as the EU's flag, anthem, and motto. It is not surprising that the citizens rejected this artificial creation of new symbols. The EU has always been, as we saw earlier, a creature that is incomparable to the nation state. It is not based on a shared past between all Europeans. For that, the history, customs, language, and lifestyle of someone living in Turku are simply too different from someone living in Sofia or Luxembourg. The EU can only offer something that binds all those citizens if it is based on a shared *future*. Only a collective aspiration for the future can hold together a continent that is so diverse. However, even this vision of Europe—as being, fundamentally, about our collective future—requires symbols.

This proposal suggests the creation of such a symbol: a new public holiday for all Europeans. On this day, we celebrate the future. Perhaps we could settle on a day in early spring, which seems a moment particularly well-suited to celebrate the future. This *Day for the Future* is *not* a celebration of Europe, or of the EU. It is, more than anything else, a moment to realise that the future is ours to create. The wonderful thing about celebrating the future, after all, is that it does not call for a moment of contemplation, but for *action*. The actions of today, after all, will shape the future.

The sole reason why certain politicians can inspire a whole generation is because they offer a convincing account of a possible future that is better, fairer, or more just. The reason why novels and TV-series that paint a dystopic picture of the future have never gone out of fashion is because they show how certain actions, big or small, can lead to a world that is barely recognisable. Halting our daily lives for one day a year and think about our individual and collective future is not just an extra holiday, it is *necessary*. The realisation that our future is contingent, that is, that our decisions today have an impact on the kind of world that we can have in 20 or 50 years, is the starting point for citizens to come together and actually create that future.

The *Day for the Future* is not, however, only about the future of our societies. It is not only about the big picture of creating a future in which, say, technological progress allows for a sustainable and egalitarian life for all citizens. The future, after all, can be about anything. And, turning this around, everything has a future: from cycling to architecture, from bird-spotting to language, and from food to computer games or classical music. The *Day for the Future* would celebrate both small and big ideas about the future, in a way that is accessible for all.

On the *Day for the Future*, the EU funds festivals throughout Europe that celebrate the future in all sort of forms. Every five years one country could host a European exhibition that brings together the most exciting, innovative, and technologically advanced projects from around Europe for its citizens to marvel at. Much like in the nineteenth and first half of the twentieth centuries, when the World Exposition brought us revolutionary images of the future and buildings such as the Eiffel Tower, the Atomium, or the Crystal Palace, host countries could receive a fund to build—literally—visions of our future. While it may not (yet) have the iconic stature of the above examples, buildings such as *Amager Bakke* in Copenhagen, *de Markthal* in Rotterdam, the *Jardin del Turia* in Valencia, or the new *Tribunal de Justice* in Paris offer this type of bold and striking reimaginations of what recycling plants, modern shopping, public parks, and the justice system could look like in the future. Each of these is revolutionary in how they imagine the future, how interactions between people might be changed by architecture, and how our communal objectives might be met in the future.

Like every holiday, the *Day for the Future* will develop its own rituals. Perhaps school kids will write a message to themselves that a website will automatically send to them in 20 years. Perhaps futuristic or dystopian movies will be released on that day. Perhaps it will supplant New Year's Eve as the moment to make resolutions for the future. Perhaps it will become the day around which children spend a day at their parent's workplace or the day when people fast in awareness of the ecological effect of modern-day consumption. Perhaps it will create none of the above rituals.

The purpose of the events that take place on the *Day of the Future*, however, is not just to have fun and create new symbols or rituals. Its subliminal message, that the future is something that is constructed by those living in the present, comes closer to a motto for the EU than anything ever has. Making explicit that whatever happens to European integration is in the hands of its citizens must be the premise for the EU's survival over the coming decades.

Estimated Costs
The cost of funding festivals throughout Europe depends on how many we would like to set up. If we allocate €5 per person for this, it would make a budget of €2.5 billion to set up all sorts of events that celebrate the future of our society and our passions—whatever they might be. If we allocate extra resources for hosting a European-wide festival each five years, with money set aside for a bold infrastructural statement of the future, this sum could rise to around €3.5 billion per year (taking as examples the costs of the buildings listed earlier),[15] which would currently be around 2.11% of the EU's budget.

FINAL REFLECTIONS

This book started with me sitting in the *Haus der Berliner Festspiele*, and feeling a rising frustration at what the EU was becoming. Writing this book has alleviated part of the frustration that I felt, all those years ago. It made me think about my own understanding of what Europe is, what the EU should be, and how we can get there. This has been a very cathartic exercise: having to explicitly engage in the construction of our collective future has been eye-opening. Like many of my contemporaries, I had never been particularly politically active. Most of us grew up in relative wealth, in prosperous countries, and with enough food, entertainment, and adventures to forget about the bigger picture. Millennials, in fact, had until recently been the least politically active generation in the past century. All this has changed because of the economic crisis, the refugee crisis, and Brexit. All of a sudden it has become clear that the stable and friendly world that we grew up in might not endure the rest of our lives. We might be the generation that sees war in Europe again. We might be the generation that deals with devastating consequences of climate change. Or we might be neither.

One thing is clear: Europe is lost. It is like a teenager—not really sure what's happening to it, a bit unclear about what the future holds for her, reminiscing about her happy youth, and caught between all-out rebellion and conformism. It's, as we all know, an uneasy and unstable state to be in. This book has tried to figure out why Europe is so lost. It has highlighted that behind the immediate crises that surround it—the economic crisis, the refugee crisis, and Brexit—another problem lurks. This is the problem of how to make collective decisions where there is disagreement between the different Member States. The current way in which the EU does this has led to a rapid increase in dissatisfaction among the Member States and the citizens, and is generating endemic distrust—on which parties from the extreme left and extreme right are capitalising.

Any regeneration of the project of European integration has to start by thinking about where this distrust comes from, and how it can be turned around. As we discussed, trust among European citizens is actually not the problem. Arguably, trust between Europeans has never been higher: we know more about each other than ever before, we cooperate more extensively than ever before, and we meet each other every day. The problem, rather, is how the EU is translating this trust between Europeans. The EU still operates on the presumption that similarity between Europeans is *the* thing that stabilises European integration. This is where the obsession with the creation of some sort of European identity comes from. Instead, as we saw, the exact opposite is the case. If anything stabilises cooperation between very diverse parts of Europe, it is respect for the differences between them.

The EU's relentless pursuit of uniformity throughout Europe and its almost pavlovian suspicion of differences between regions in Europe come, it must be said, from a good place. The EU was deliberately designed to do this. It was designed, in 1957, to achieve peace and prosperity. Peace meant trying to limit differences and antagonism between its Member States, and prosperity meant tying their economies together in a single market—where the same rules apply to everyone. It is without doubt a measure of the EU's success that it is now seen as something that threatens local diversity and isn't sufficiently sensitive to what citizens want from it. As the threats of war and economic collapse have subsided over the past six decades, however, it has left the EU in a bit of an uneasy—somewhat teenage—state: now what do we do?

Perhaps the best description about where we find ourselves in the process of European integration today comes from the Canadian band Arcade Fire. Their song *Culture War* starts with the following lines: '*Now the future is staring at me/like a vision of the past/and I know these crumbs they've sold me/they're never going to last*'. As the younger generations of Europeans stare into our collective future, all we see is an image of the future as it was thought up in 1957. And what is left of that image—the few crumbs that can still enthuse Europeans and hold the project of European integration together are, needless to say, not going to last much longer.

But changing the very purpose of the project of European integration is easier said than done. If we want the EU to—once again—become a project that speaks to our collective future, it will require a thorough renovation. Only by transforming it into something that the citizens can control, can we ensure that the EU remains an institutional echo of what it means to be European, today and tomorrow. The radicalism involved in this exercise cannot be overstated. This is not like changing the lay-out of your living room, or giving the bathroom a lick of paint. This is more like a teenager struggling to find out who she really is, and they deciding to explicitly express that identity. It will be chaotic, it will be messy, and it will be unpredictable. But it is a period that the EU—like all of us—has to go through to become something else.

So now it's up to us. It is up to all Europeans to think about the kind of young adult that the teenager EU should become. Whichever vision of the future of Europe you think has merit, now, more than ever before, is the time to start engaging with it. Because the single best thing about the future is that it hasn't happened yet!

NOTES

1. Munich Security Report 2018, available at: https://www.securityconference.de/en/publications/munich-security-report
2. http://www.youdiscover.eu/
3. Eurostat Tourism Statistics, available at: https://ec.europa.eu/eurostat/statistics-explained/index.php/Tourism_statistics#Tourism_participation:_EU_residents_make_1.2_billion_trips
4. N. Srnicek and A. Williams, *Inventing the Future: Postcapitalism and a World without Work* (Verso, 2016) 86.
5. P. Van Parijs & Y. Vanderborght, *Basic Income* (Harvard University Press, 2017).
6. See for a detailed overview, chapter 6 of P. Van Parijs & Y. Vanderborght, *Basic Income* (Harvard University Press, 2017).
7. https://www.forbes.com/sites/kittyknowles/2018/05/02/station-f-is-the-worlds-biggest-startup-incubator-could-it-also-become-the-best/#93e126562d0c
8. R. Sennett, *Together: The Rituals, Pleasures and Politics of Cooperation* (Penguin, 2013), 82.
9. EEA Technical Report 6/2009, *Europe's Onshore and Offshore wind energy potential: an assessment of environmental and economic constraints*. Available at: https://www.eea.europa.eu/publications/europes-onshore-and-offshore-wind-energy-potential
10. Special Eurobarometer 459 on Climate Change (2017.4763), available at: https://ec.europa.eu/clima/sites/clima/files/support/docs/report_2017_en.pdf
11. With a massive thanks to Alasdair Graham for helping me with these calculations.
12. https://www.drawdown.org/solutions/electricity-generation/wind-turbines-onshore
13. Volkskrant, 13 March 2016, available at: https://www.volkskrant.nl/mensen/kinderen-op-school-een-warme-lunch-goed-idee-~b28942cc/
14. http://www.schoolfoodplan.com/wp-content/uploads/2013/07/School-Food-Plan-2013.pdf, p. 124.
15. The Rotterdam *Markthal* cost €178 million, *Amager Bakke* cost €578 million, and both the *Tribunal de Justice* in Paris and Calatrava's reinvention of the Valencian riverbed cost around €800 million.

INDEX

© The Author(s) 2020
F. de Witte, *re:generation Europe*,
https://doi.org/10.1007/978-3-030-19788-9